THE LONG ISLAND RAILROAD POLICE DEPARTMENT

The Police of New York City

robert l. bryan

Published by robert l. bryan, 2023.

THE LONG ISLAND RAILROAD POLICE DEPARTMENT

First edition. July 27, 2023.

Copyright © 2023 robert l. bryan.

ISBN: 979-8223420446

Written by robert l. bryan.

For Meghan

Prologue:

In just the third book in this series about obscure and obsolete police departments that operated in New York City, I fear I may have stirred up some controversy. If you are one of the millions of people who have read this book (a man can fantasize, can't he?), you may have thrown the book down and said, "Wait just a minute. What is this guy trying to pull on us? I wanted to read a book about cops in New York City and he's giving me Long Island."

For those lodging such a protest, let me explain. True, the vast majority of the Long Island Railroad's tracks are located outside of New York City, in the counties of Nassau and Suffolk, but the heart of the operation, including the police operations, was within the city. Penn Station in Manhattan, Jamaica Station in Queens and the Flatbush Avenue Terminal in Brooklyn were the hubs of operations for the LIRR Police Department. Even before Penn Station existed and the Greater City of New York did not exist before 1898, the Long Island Railroad and its police operations were centered around Long Island City in the borough of Queens.

Now that I have hopefully squashed the controversy to your satisfaction, I hope you enjoy the story of the Long Island Railroad Police Department.

Introduction:

Maryland and South Carolina were the first states to build railroads in the early 1830's. By 1835, Kentucky, Tennessee, Alabama, Indiana, Louisiana, Ohio, Michigan and Illinois were part of the eleven states with over 200 railroads and approximately 1000 miles of main line track. The railroads had over 9000 miles of main line by 1850, all in the eastern states. In 1851 the railroads crossed the Mississippi and began their expansion westward. By 1860 there were over 30,000 miles of railroad establishing boomtowns, settlers, and adventure seekers in their path.

With the creation of these railroad towns, crime tended to follow. There were no railroad police at that time, and usually no other forms of law enforcement. Vigilante groups were usually organized haphazardly to maintain law and order. These groups were not very productive causing the railroads to fall prey to criminals looking to steal luggage, freight, and livestock from the trains.

Chief Engineer Benjamin Latrobe of the Baltimore and Ohio Railroad established one of the earliest known railroad police forces in 1849. With the assistance of Sheriff J. F. Martin of Acting Preston County (now West Virginia), they arrested the leaders of strikers who were assaulting other workers. This gave Latrobe the idea of creating his own railroad police force, one hired and paid entirely by the railroad. It was decided that these men would be deputized by Preston County so that all of their official acts would be covered under the shield of law.

Latrobe's force would be made up of twelve men responsible for keeping workers in line while the railroads continued their expansion. Each man would be paid $1.25 a day with the instructions to "arrest persons engaged in riotous acts, dead or alive."

Later that year, Latrobe's police force led by John Watson saw their first real action at the Kingwood Tunnel construction site. They met over 200 rioting strikers who had shot at workers in the twin coal mine shafts. Watson and his men opened fire and charged the strikers, driving them away. Other teams of Watson's men saw action against violent strikers in Cumberland, Maryland and Wheeling, West Virginia.

Most railroads prior to the Civil War still did not have their own police force or one experienced with undercover work and investigations. As losses mounted, railroads had a need to protect themselves against well-organized criminals. Contractors were hired to investigate the losses to freight and luggage that were mounting into the millions of dollars. One of these contractors and probably the most famous one was Allen Pinkerton. He used his men and women in many ways to solve thefts from the railroads. He placed them in undercover capacity as passengers watching for employees who were stealing and as conductors and other employees watching for those stealing from passengers or tramps. One such undercover agent used by Pinkerton was James McParland who worked as a conductor watching for pickpockets and thieves. He was later successfully used against the "Molly Maguires" who were burning bridges, destroying rail cars, and committing other railroad related crimes.

Allan Pinkerton was born in Glasgow, Scotland, the son of a police officer. He migrated to the United States in 1842 after working as a barrel maker for some years. While working in Illinois as a woodchopper, he assisted the local police department with apprehending a gang of counterfeiters. His thirst for law enforcement had begun and soon after was employed by the Kane County, Illinois Sheriff's Office. Pinkerton later went to work for the Chicago Police Department becoming their very first Detective.

Only two years after making Detective, he quit the Chicago Police Department to sign a contract with the Rock Island, the Galena & Chicago Union Railroads (the latter to be incorporated into the Chicago & North Western Railroad), and the Illinois Central Railroads. This contract called for his company to exclusively work on railroad related crimes. He established his railroad investigative business under the name of the Northwestern Police Detective Agency later renamed Pinkerton's National Detective Agency. This agency was the first of its kind with their agents having the power to arrest criminals anywhere in the country.

As the Civil War came to an end, the railroads were used to lead the fast-paced economic growth throughout the country. They turned small towns into business hubs, some workers into wealthy entrepreneurs, and others into bandits. As the railroads continued to grow westward the American Outlaw began to rob and steal from passengers, freight cars, and express cars. In their daring robberies, these American Outlaws were well manned and well-armed. They overpowered crews, dynamited bridges, tunnels, stations, tracks, and rail cars making away with thousands of dollars, jewelry and other freight. One of the most successful and easiest ways to stop a train, however, was simply to wave a red lantern in front of the train flagging it to a stop. During many of these robberies, there were shootouts where passengers and employees of the railroads were killed. This began the era of the outlaw, Jesse and Frank James, the Youngers, Reno and Dalton Brothers, Sam Bass, Belle Star, and others.

On October 6, 1866, the first known train robbery took place. Three masked bandits boarded an Ohio & Mississippi train after it departed Seymour, Indiana. John and Simeon Reno and Franklin Sparks knocked the guard unconscious before pushing two safes containing a total $45,000 out of the moving train and making their escape.

Allan Pinkerton was immediately called to investigate this robbery. His knowledge of the territory was instrumental in solving this case. He knew that nothing happened around Seymour without the knowledge or approval of the Reno brothers. Pinkerton immediately used undercover agents on this case. Dick Winscott, one of Pinkerton's best agents, was working as a bartender where the Reno brothers did their drinking and gambling. One evening when John Reno and Sparks were drinking, Winscott talked them into getting their picture taken by a photographer who had just happened to walk into the bar. They agreed to this by having the photographer, one of Pinkerton's other agents, take their picture. This picture was then sent immediately to Pinkerton's office and was used to successfully identify them as the robbers of the train.

During the outlaw era of the 1860's, the railroads realized the need for their own police departments. It was usually the division superintendents or the operating managers who did the hiring and firing of the police department. These were not the times for timid men; railroad police were big, strong and aggressive men who could defend themselves. Many railroad agents would engage in gun battles with the outlaws with some losing their life trying to protect railroad employees, passengers and goods.

The railroads also realized that they needed to protect the employees and freight in the rail yards from the less sophisticated thief. To combat this problem, they began to hire watchmen. Many times, watchmen were employees from other crafts who were unsuitable for the jobs they held. There was no training for these men. They were handed a gun, badge and a club and told to go out and protect the railroad property and employees. The railroad watchman was not of the quality of men and women that Allan Pinkerton hired for railroad investigation. As railroads police agencies were in their infant stages, they still called on Allan Pinkerton and his sons to handle many of their investigations.[1]

The Long Island Railroad is one of the oldest and most famous rail networks in the US, having been in operation since 1834. The LIRR has existed since before the Statue of Liberty and the American Civil War and still runs today, having survived two World Wars, a number of bankruptcies, hurricanes and countless takeovers. Still operating under its original name and charter, the oldest railroad in the US has become a major institution for the region and one of the few services in the country to operate 24/7, all year long.

A state-owned commuter network running from the heart of Manhattan to eastern part of Suffolk County on Long Island, the LIRR today connects 124 stations along over 700 miles of track. It serves about 81 million commuters a year. Now property of the New York State Metropolitan Transportation Authority (MTA), the railroad was originally born as a private franchise in the 1830s. Initially meant to be called the Brooklyn & Jamaica (B&J) Railroad Company – after the names of the two areas it was built to connect, Jamaica in Queens and Brooklyn– the service was the first rail network ever built on Long Island.

An immediate problem had to do with the line's structure, which stretched towards the center of Long Island, a scarcely populated area that offered far fewer opportunities than the coastline in terms of both passengers and freight. Adding to that, the LIRR suffered a substantial blow in 1848, when the opening of a rail route connecting New York and Boston through Connecticut (also known as the New York and New Haven Railroad) challenged the LIRR's very reason for existence. Incapable of competing with New York and New Haven Railroad, the LIRR was forced to declare bankruptcy. But this wasn't the end of the LIRR, which managed to survive the crisis by turning its focus to local passenger services and expanding its reach to Long Island's more densely populated areas.

Between the 1850s and 1870s, this was made possible through the acquisition of several smaller franchises, including the New York & Flushing Railroad and prime competitor the Central Railroad of Long Island. In addition, new business opportunities came from the City of Brooklyn. After years of friction over its ban on the use of steam engines, the route eventually became part of the LIRR's services.

The year 1880 was marked by the arrival of Austin Corbin, a robber baron from New Hampshire, whose takeover of the LIRR started a year of great prosperity for the service. Under his leadership, a second line reaching the southern shore of the Atlantic Ocean was completed, while the network further expanded to destinations including Manhattan Beach, Long Beach and Port Washington. Corbin also managed to buy out all of the line's main competitors, making the LIRR the only rail service on Long Island.

The turn of the century brought a new owner to the LIRR, which was sold to the Pennsylvania Railroad (PRR) for $6m. The move was part of the PRR's expansion bid, which meant to improve commuter services across New York and the nearby region. The construction of Pennsylvania (Penn) Station, in Manhattan, in 1901, was a key factor in achieving this purpose. Under the PRR, nearly 30% of the Long Island Rail Road's network was electrified. Its brand-new all-steel cars carried over 800 passengers a day during the summer and just under 750 during the winter season.

This period of prosperity eventually came to an end, as a number of factors – from a decline in services during the Second World War to an increase in taxes between the 1920s and 1940s – damaged the service, which was also facing toughening competition with New York's new subway system. These issues culminated in 1946, when the PRR posted losses for the first time in its history and, having let go of the LIRR, left it to deal with a new bankruptcy.

In the 1950s, the growing lack of funds and separation for the PRR had a particularly damaging impact on the service's aging equipment and infrastructure. The company's declining reputation was further hit when a series of accidents on its line killed 115 people.

In the midst of this decline, the State of New York came to the LIRR's rescue as it began subsidizing the line throughout the 1960s. During this period, the state invested around $60m in new rolling stock, locomotives and infrastructure upgrades that kept the line running. The LIRR was eventually acquired by the State of New York's newly formed Metropolitan Transport Authority, which kicked off further modernization projects in the following decades.

A revamped Penn Station is the MTA's most notable product of the 1990s, when Governor George Pataki launched extensive works to redecorate it, expand it and introduce air conditioning throughout the hub. During these years, the MTA also decided to sell the LIRR's freight division to the New York and Atlantic Railway after witnessing a 25-year drop in freight operations on Long Island.

At the dawn of the new millennium, the operator also began works on its East Side Access project, which entailed extending the mainline towards the east side of Manhattan via Grand Central Terminal. However, the project, which officially launched in 2007, has been continuously hit by delays and cost increases. Now scheduled to be completed in 2022, it will be partially funded by the MTA's capital plan announced earlier this year.[2]

As far as policing on the Long Island Railroad, 1868 is listed as the year the Long Island Railroad Police Department was formed.

1868 – 1899:

Although the LIRR Police Department was established in 1868, the first documented police action I could find was in 1885. Captain Woods, who was also referred to as the chief of the LIRR Police Department, took custody of a young woman who was acting strangely and risking injury to herself at Hunter's Point. Woods observed the female jumping on and off trains while they were in motion, skipping around the platform and nearly falling under the wheels of a car.

At the station house the girl gave her name as Sarah Curran, but would not reveal her home address, other than to say it was in New York City. The only name she would provide as a contact was Sexton Hart, of the Roman Catholic Cathedral in New York City. Captain Woods telegraphed the sexton and was able to piece together a story. It appeared that Ms. Curran had been employed as a domestic in a hotel on Long Beach. A day earlier, the manager of the hotel found her work unacceptable and placed her on an LIRR train to New York City. When she arrived at Hunter's Point she sent a telegram to Mr. Southgate at the Long Beach hotel, advising him that she was returning to the hotel. She then purchased a ticket but up until Captain Woods found her, she spent the time skipping around the platform jumping on and off trains.[3]

This was not the only reference I found involving Captain Woods. On September 2, 1885, the Captain was involved in a much more problematic incident. George Jacobs, a New York City resident, obtained a warrant for the arrest of Captain Woods on the charge of assault in the third degree. It appeared that three days earlier Jacobs was going to Rockaway and purchased tickets for all his family except for one very young son. After Jacobs had his family seated in the car, Captain Woods entered and ordered Jacobs to go back to the ticket office and purchase a ticket for the little boy. Jacobs refused so Captain Woods ejected him from the car. In ejecting him, Jacobs alleged that

Woods used unnecessary force and would have clubbed him if his children had not begged the Captain to stop. Captain Woods said he did not use excessive force and never pulled out his club. He said he was merely enforcing one of the rules of the railroad.[4]

The next day Jacobs appeared in court using the name George Van Dyke and attempted to obtain another arrest warrant for Captain Woods. The complaint was the same in that he alleged that Woods had dragged him out of the car inflicting serious injuries upon his person. Justice Kavanagh recognized the complainant as the same person who a few weeks earlier had alleged he had been robbed in a gambling house in Hunter's Point. He failed to prove his case and it was concluded that he intended to blackmail the proprietor of the establishment.[5] The next day Justice Kavanagh dismissed all charges against Captain Woods.[6]

There has always been a degree of risk in police work, even back in the 19th century. On the night of June 6, 1886, LIRR Officer Murray was assaulted and seriously injured by four men. Anton Novak, John Serk, Kohn Kilion, and Victor Klar had attended a picnic in Adams' Park and were smoking cigarettes while waiting for a train on the Woodside station. Officer Murray requested that they not smoke on the station, at which point they began to beat Murray on the head with canes loaded with lead. Officer Murray recovered fully from his head injuries.[7]

In the 19th century liquor was a big police problem, as many of the incidents officers responded to were related to drinking in some way. On August 28,, 1888, Kate Healy, a middle aged woman from Long Island was taken into custody for being drunk on the train as it arrived at Hunter's Point. Healy said she was making her way home to Ireland because she had finally saved up enough money to spend the rest of her life in peace in her native country. When she was arraigned, Justice Kavanagh noted that she did not appear to be a woman with a drinking problem before releasing her and wishing her luck on her journey home.

John Sheehy had been on the same station but was a completely different case. Sheehy had been working as a laborer on the railroad and had come to Hunter's Point to receive his pay. With money in his pocket he proceeded to get extremely drunk and when he returned to the station he became very loud and belligerent. Officer Marinan approached Sheehy and warned him to behave himself and to stop swearing. Sheehy said, "Go to blazes! I've sworn since I was a boy and I'm not going to stop."

The officer did not have any trouble taking Sheehy into custody when a commuter passing by punched Sheehy behind the ear while another struck him in the eye. With Sheehy instantly subdued Officer Marinan took him into custody where instead of receiving best wishes on a trip to Ireland, he received five days in jail.[8]

The 19th century LIRR police force was mainly a compilation of constables, special officers and watchman. There were even special deputy sheriff's working for the railroad police force. In 1893 Special Deputy Sheriff Thomas Hartz had a lively tussle one night with several passengers on the 9:10 Rockaway Beach train to Long Island City. The train was crowded, and several passengers stood on the platform between cars. While the train was crossing Jamaica Bay, Hartz ordered John Blair and James Lahay to come back inside the car. Blair and Lahey must have been comfortable riding between cars because they refused the order and a rough and tumble fight ensued, in which the train crew joined in to help the deputy sheriff. Many passengers in the car joined in the fray and several women were injured. When the train pulled into Long Island City everyone went about their business as if nothing had happened. I guess that's how they did things in the Gay 90's.[9]

Theft of railroad equipment always has and always will be an issue for the Long Island Railroad. In 1899 track fittings valued at several thousand dollars were stolen. The thieves were arrested after a dramatic chase across the meadows in Edgemere during which several gunshots were exchanged before the crooks surrendered. The pursuit was led by Chief Detective James Sarvis, who was identified as the head of the LIRR Police Department. Throughout the early history of the LIRR Police Department, I discovered that several titles were used to identify the top spot. Before Chief Detective Sarvis, Captain Woods had been in charge. Later, I would find the title superintendent being used to identify the chief of the department.[10]

Sarvis worked diligently against the railroad thieves, and he succeeded in arresting a man who was believed to be behind numerous thefts of LIRR property in Queens and Nassau counties. For several weeks Sarvis and his detectives tracked down the thief who had been stealing metal pieces of railroad cars as they sat in sidings at various locations. One of the clues Sarvis utilized was the fact that there were always burglaries committed of homes in the area where the railroad thefts occurred. The southside villages between Springfield and Freeport appeared to be the crook's favorite field of operation. Sarvis watched this area very closely and looked for two strange men who were often seen riding around in a peddler's cart in the vicinity of the crimes. Sarvis and his crew maintained surveillance for several nights until the peddler's wagon appeared. Sarvis followed the wagon and caught Otto Eckholdt, an anarchist from Maspeth, in the act of loading metal pieces of a rail car in his cart. Sarvis arrested Eckholdt and lodged him in the jail in Long Island City.[11]

Another case that added to Sarvis' reputation involved the wealthy Hyatt family, who lived in an estate at Newtown. Sarvis saw a trunk on one of the railroad baggage trucks one afternoon. It bore the initials H.B.H. and the word Newtown. The letters had been scraped in an effort to remove them. Sarvis knew that the Hyatt family was in Europe, so he took custody of the trunk and the men who had it and traveled to Newtown where he captured the other members of the gang who were inside the Hyatt house. One of the thieves confessed and led Sarvis to a lonely place in a patch of woods, where he dug up silverware and other valuables the thieves had buried. The gang had removed much of the furniture from the home and had even sold the piano. While Sarvis was at the house a truck drove up to remove the piano he had purchased. The thieves received long jail terms.[12]

19th century newspaper depiction of an LIRR robbery

A CLOSE WATCH KEPT FOR PICKPOCKETS.

Newspaper depiction of a brawl inside an LIRR train

James Sarvis – Chief of LIRR Police

1900 – 1919:

Frederick De Bosche was the model police officer. After fifteen years with the Long Island Railroad Police Department, Special Policeman De Bosche was an expert at his trade. He worked steadily at the main depot in Long Island City where the duties were different from those of a patrolman on the street. De Bosche was known to thousands of patrons of the railroad system and was a special friend to women and children who were unaccustomed to travel and feared getting on the wrong train. Like all railroad policemen, De Bosche had to answer hundreds of questions at the same time by people crowding around him. He had to know every point on the road and the easiest way to reach it. The railroad provided a Bureau of Information to help customers, but people always seemed to run to the first policeman they saw. De Bosche always dealt with people with patience and a smile on his face, no matter how hectic the situation became.

On the morning of May 1, 1903, De Bosche was on his post when he heard screams coming from the direction of the East River. When the officer reached the edge of the river, he observed a small boy struggling to stay afloat in the water. Without a moment of hesitation De Bosche jumped into the river in full uniform, including his helmet. He pulled the boy out of the river, and once the 8-year-old was safe, De Bosche walked home, changed into a dry uniform and returned to his post without ever reporting his actions. Chief Sarvis only learned about the rescue from an outsider. That's modesty![13]

James Sarvis died in 1905 after being in charge of the Long Island Railroad Police Department since 1890. He was a top crimefighter who was credited with many clever arrests during his fifteen years with the LIRR and eight years with the New York police force. Sarvis was also a very colorful character, once stating that he was on speaking terms with almost every rich man in America. He was 61 when he passed away.[14]

The death of James Sarvis ushered in sweeping changes to the Long Island Railroad Police Department. LIRR President Ralph Peters decided that the handful of special officers, deputy sheriffs and watchmen were not sufficient to protect the interests of the thousands of commuters, as well as the property being shipped by the railroad. The result was a complete reorganization of a new police force consisting of 400 men with the promise of more men to be added. There seemed to be some confusion about the manpower number. Some records did reflect the manpower being 400, but I found several documents that indicated the new force consisted of 200 personnel. Throughout the lifespan of the LIRR Police Department, the manpower never rose much above 200, so I would tend to think 400 was either a mistake or an exaggeration.

Robert E. Kerkam was made Superintendent of Police. Kerkam was born in Pennsylvania in 1857. He entered the military in 1878, serving among the Native Americans on the western frontier, between the British possessions and Colorado, after which he was transferred to Washington D.C. where his promotion was rapid until 1886 when he became assistant to the Secretary of Agriculture of Illinois. He held several military and civilian government positions until 1897, when he left the government service and became connected with the Long Island Railroad in various capacities. His positions went from clerk in the auditor's office to pay clerk and timekeeper of the transportation department, then to chief clerk to the general superintendent, and by successive steps to the chief clerk to the president from where he was promoted to Superintendent of Police.

The new police department was originally so successful that it was rumored that Manhattan officials had their eyes on Kerkam as a possible candidate to run the New York Police Department.

The new police department was modelled after the system on the Pennsylvania Railroad lines, with Kerkam spending time studying that system prior to accepting the promotion to superintendent.

The Department was divided into four sections, with two lieutenants in immediate control and in touch with numerous patrolmen and crossing watchmen on day and night duty in each section.

First Division: The north shore, extending from the ferries to Whitestone Landing and to Port Washington.

Second Division: Covered by the main line and Montauk Division, between Long Island City and Jamaica, north of the Atlantic Division.

Third Division: The Atlantic, Manhattan Beach and Rockaway Divisions.

Fourth Division: The district east of Jamaica, covering the Oyster Bay, Wading River, main line and Montauk Divisions.

The new police headquarters was Long Island City and was staffed by the superintendent, one inspector, one captain and four lieutenants, with two freight and express investigators. Another headquarters at East New York had one captain and two lieutenants while two lieutenants at Jamaica reported to the captain at East New York

The uniformed force, including those having special authority as special patrolmen from the New York City Commissioner of Police, numbered about fifty men. Those men working within the limits of Brooklyn and Queens were sworn in as special patrolmen for New York City. Those men performing duty in Nassau and Suffolk counties were appointed special deputy sheriffs. This uniformed force wore uniforms similar to those worn by the New York Police Department.

Crossing watchmen and some patrolmen not requiring a full uniform were issued a five pointed star badge bearing the wording, "Police Service, L.I.R.R.." They were also supplied with a corduroy cap bearing the wording, "Crossing Watchman, L.I.R.R.," on a nickeled plate on the front of the cap. There were other members of the patrol force who did not wear uniforms. There was a non-uniformed squad detailed to protect the electrical equipment and patrol electrified third rails and transmission lines. These officers did not wear uniforms but did carry badges.

Since all employees of the police service were required to submit regular reports on all activities on their posts, recruiting of police personnel looked for men of intelligence with at least a basic education.

The specific requirements for this new LIRR police force were as follows:

- Age between 21 and 35
- Height between 5 feet 8 inches and 6 feet 2 inches
- Weight between 160 and 200 pounds
- All applicants had to pass a medical exam
- All applicants had to be able to read and write English [15]

One of the first results of the police reorganization was the cleaning out of tipsters and rowdies on racetrack trains. For years, those traveling to the racetrack in Sheepshead Bay had been bothered by unsavory characters who defied watchmen and train crews and pursued their rowdy behavior in the cars and terminals. After the racing scene shifted from Saratoga to Sheepshead Bay, Superintendent Kerkam stationed policemen at the terminals and sent plainclothes men through cars, with the result that the patrons of race trains were unmolested. Additionally, the annoying whistling and singing by some on the race trains was suppressed. Finally, smokers were relegated to the head end of the trains.

The existing crossing watchmen welcomed the reorganization of the department. There were many more crossing watchmen employed and they were now allowed to wear a badge of office. Most importantly, the new police department gave the crossing watchman a future. In the past, the crossing watchman ended where he began. There was no career path, and some railroad records revealed some watchman remaining in the same job for over fifty years. Superintendent Kerkam discovered that many of the crossing watchmen were lively and intelligent young men, worthy of the opportunity to work themselves into regular patrolman duties where they could earn even further advancement.

According to Superintendent Kerkam, the philosophy of the new LIRR Police Department was to protect rather than detect. Policemen would report any train that was overcrowded and cooperate with the transportation department to see that there was a seat for every passenger. Policemen were ordered to keep a strict watch along the lines with the idea of preventing possible accidents before they occurred.

There was no doubt at the time that the new police force was here to stay. Not only did an efficient police department add to the status of the railroad, but because of the higher protection afforded to passengers and property, it saved the railroad thousands of dollars a year.[16]

Superintendent Kerkam's new profession force received an immediate black eye with an incident that occurred in the Jamaica Yard. Larry Bundy was a police department watchman assigned to the Jamaica Yard who was not well liked by the workers in the yard. Larry wasn't the very friendly type, but the hostility towards him was mainly due to his insistence of following the rules that required seals to be placed on car doors as soon as they were closed even though the car was only going to be moved a very short distance within the yard.

One evening, a group of freight train employees in the yard thought it would be great fun to scare Larry, so they rigged up a dummy to make it look like a man in the process of breaking open a freight car. The popular belief was that besides being surly, Larry was also a coward, so the crew in the yard believed Larry would tune and run when he saw a thief in the process of breaking into the car.

The yard crew knew which direction Larry would be coming from, so once the dummy was in place, they hid themselves around the opposite corner of the car and waited. A few minutes later Larry approached, and the plan worked like a charm – sort of. The dummy completely fooled Larry, but he did not run away at the sight of a thief breaking into a car. Instead, he stood his ground and drew his revolver, shouting for the crook to put his hands in the air and slowly turn. Naturally, there was no response from the thief, and when Larry thought he saw a gun in the man's hand, Larry poured a fusillade of bullets into the criminal. In all, 12 of the 14 bullets Larry fired found their mark in the dummy. The hidden pranksters were the only ones running away when they found Larry's barrage of bullets coming uncomfortably close to where they were hiding. It was said that after that night no one in the Jamaica Yard ever complained about having to seal a car again.[17]

Superintendent Kerkam's new force saved the railroad money immediately when detectives uncovered a ticket scam. When Kerkam became aware of the allegation of irregularities with ticket sales, he assigned detectives to ride back and forth on trains copying the numbers of the tickets they purchased at different stations and noting how the tickets were treated by the gatemen and collectors. The detectives had to utilize great discretion during the operation to prevent those engaged in the plot from discovering they were being watched.

The detectives determined that on many occasions, tickets were not being punched when they were collected on the trains. The tickets were then returned to be sold a second time, and sometimes three and four times. The LIRR had no idea how much money was stolen because there was no way to determine how many times the tickets were sold. The consensus, however, was that the financial loss was substantial. The railroad did not want to wait and lose more money while building evidence, so no criminal charges were filed, but the suspected employees were terminated.[18]

In November of 1905 Kerkam's philosophy of prevention was put to the test at the Aqueduct station. Police Officer Jacob Warner was posted at the station protecting the traveling public from the electrified third rail adjacent to the tracks. Some members of the public apparently did not appreciate the officer's protective actions. Five young men disputed Warner's authority to tell them what to do. They picked up railroad spikes and bricks and attempted to assault Warner as he tried to place them under arrest. When they began to run Warner fired two shots at 21-year-old Nathan Ryan, who was hit in the right leg. Other police officers responded and arrested two other men. Ryan and his two accomplices were charged with assault.[19]

In 1909 Superintendent Kerkam listed the police department's manpower at 350. He said that since the newly organized department had been in operation for a few years, the positive results reached beyond the railroad. The crooks did not confine their criminal activities to the property of the railroad, and in investigating criminal activity on the railroad it often led to evidence of crimes off the railroad. On many occasions horses and wagons stolen from merchants and farmers were recovered by LIRR police officers. Through the railroad officers knowledge of the identities and techniques of criminals who frequented Long Island, Long Island Railroad Police were responsible for thwarting robberies of banks, post offices, and other mercantile establishments. Additionally, there were times when railroad police were in good position to arrest criminals who were escaping after committing crimes.

Kerkam explained that the department in 1909 was structured with a day and night captain, as well as a captain in charge of the fire service. There were two day and two night lieutenants and four day and four night roundsmen.

The superintendent also disclosed some of the rules his officers worked under:

• The use of intoxicants while on duty was prohibited.

• The use of firearms save as a last resort to prevent personal injury was prohibited. It was better to let an offender escape than by a reckless use of a deadly weapon to inflict an injury that would render the patrolman himself legally and personally responsible.

• Patrolmen in yards or terminals in charge of yardmasters or agents had to cooperate with them at all times.

• When riding on trains they had to assist the conductor in the maintenance of order.

• Harshness or cruelty to prisoners would not be tolerated.

• Drunken persons on company property had to be removed to a place of safety.

• People throwing stones or other missiles at trains had to be arrested.

In 1909 New York State did not have a trespass law as it related to the area around railroad tracks. Superintendent Kerkam said that such a law would do away with a great number of accidents to people who persisted in walking the tracks.[20]

As time passed criminals enhanced the methods they used. Their operations included dynamiting station safes with automobiles and fast horses being used in their escapes. To keep up with the criminal techniques in 1911 the Long Island Railroad Police equipped some of its patrolmen with motorcycles and bicycles – but the rate of robberies remained consistent. Recalling the good results obtained by German, English, French, and Belgian municipalities through the employment of trained dogs, Superintendent Kerkam purchased two English bloodhounds, which were immediately trained for police service. From the two dogs, six pups were bred. One of the pups died shortly after birth, but that left the LIRR Police with seven K9s.

The use of the dogs proved worthwhile. Copper bond wires were being cut on the Manhattan Beach Division, putting signals out of order, and seriously affecting train movements. Taking the scent from the cold steel rails the dogs followed the trail to an East New York liquor shop, the thief's residence, a junk dealer, and finally to the foreman of a gang of laborers who had committed the theft.

A station on the east end of Long Island was broken into and the contents of the ticket box stolen. A trace of blood was on a piece of window glass that the burglar had smashed with his hand. He walked about a mile and a half and then secured a rig. The bloodhounds trailed him, and he was captured even though he had a twelve-hour head start.

Aside from tracking railroad thieves, the dogs assisted in clearing up many burglaries and other crimes in many Long Island communities. In one case a little girl was abducted in Huntington. The entire surrounding area was searched day and night by residents and local policemen without success. Someone telephoned the Long Island Railroad Police headquarters and three hours after starting the hounds the girl was safe and her abductor was in custody.[21]

On July 26, 1911, a new crisis struck the Long Island Railroad Police Department. New York City Mayor William Jay Gaynor had become fed up with instances of untrained, unprofessional special patrolman creating incidents while working for private entities, so he issued an order cancelling the licenses of all New York City special patrolmen regardless of whether they were hired for a Sunday beer picnic in a park or by a big railroad line. That big railroad line was the LIRR who had approximately fifty men deputized as New York City special patrolmen.

Under New York City regulations, city police officers did not perform duty on the property of private corporations, so depriving the LIRR special patrolmen of their authority would leave the hundreds of thousands of men, women and children visiting summer and beach resorts at the mercy of pickpockets and thugs while on railroad property. Rockaway Beach and Coney Island and the big terminal points were among the places that were sure to be most affected.

With their trained men and pack of bloodhounds the police force on the Long Island Railroad had been keeping thieves of all sorts on the run throughout the territory they covered. Under the direction of Superintendent Kerkam, the special patrolmen in New York City cooperated at all times with the city police and gave them precedence whenever the situation demanded. LIRR police arrests had resulted in a 90% conviction rate.

Kerkam took Mayor Gaynor's move in stride and was busy arranging for the continued safeguarding of stations, crossings, yards and terminals. Kerkam respected that the Mayor was entitled to his opinion and certainly had the authority to cancel the authority of the special patrolmen. He said that about fifty of his men would be affected by the order, but that it would not impair the efficiency of the force to any great degree. Kerkam pointed out that all his men were educated in police work in the same manner as the city police, with his men obtaining additional knowledge of railroad law. Kerkam said that he understood that there were many special patrolmen employed by individuals and corporations who had no police education, and that he had previously suggested that special patrolmen should be required to pass an examination. Kerkam pointed out that the laws of the State of New York state that any citizen could make an arrest for crimes committed in their presence or for felonies not committed in their presence when the evidence pointed to the fact that a felony was committed. He admitted that his men would have to stop making arrests on the complaints of patrons for misdemeanors that were not committed in the officer's presence. Kerkam shrugged and said that he hoped the customers of the LIRR would be lenient with his men in stone throwing and petty larceny cases or when disorderly conduct was occurring on a train or terminal when no officer was present, and when the officer arrived he had to explain that he could take no action.[22]

Superintendent Kerkam's concerns became a moot point when Mayor Gaynor reconsidered his order, and the next day he amended his edict to allow officers of public transportation corporations to keep their special patrolman status.[23]

Safety was and still is an important issue on the railroad. Back in 1912 Superintendent Kerkam initiated what may have been one of the first school outreach programs to address some of the violations primarily committed by youths.

The following letter was addressed to the principals of all the schools in the villages on the North Shore Division of the Long Island Railroad:

The electrification of our North Shore Division, between Pennsylvania Station and Whitestone Landing, makes trespassing along our right of way, or playing about our stations, a very dangerous habit, and I wish you would kindly invite the attention of your scholars to this subject, as well as to the crime of stone throwing at trains, interfering with signals, placing obstructions on tracks or playing about railroad property.

Section 83 of the Railroad Law prohibits and makes it a misdemeanor for any unauthorized person to walk on or along the tracks of any railroad of this State.

Section 1991 of the Penal Law makes it a felony for any person who willfully places any obstruction on tracks of any railroad or throws stones or other missiles at a railroad train, locomotive, car or vehicle standing or moving upon the tracks.

Section 1422 of the Penal law makes it a felony for any person to interfere with or alter a signal which may lead a train into danger.

It is not desired to cause the arrest of children in cases where they sometimes do wrong through the mere lack of warning and instruction, and I am, therefore, requesting you to assist me in this matter and use your influence with your pupils to prevent a great deal of trouble in the future. Yours very truly,

R.E. KERKAM Superintendent of Police

Long Island Railroad Company

The youths of Elmhurst, Corona, Winfield, and Woodside had been particularly troublesome along those lines, especially in placing obstructions on the tracks. There was a popular belief that the new "movie" industry had contributed to the problem. One of the most exciting scenes in a motion picture involved a train wreck. In one instance several railroad ties were found across the tracks in Elmhurst, with the investigation determining that the culprits were lads with the "movie craze" who wanted to see a real train wreck.[24]

Two years later Kerkam attempted another youth outreach. This time he sent a letter to the Boy Scouts of America, asking the help of the scouts in preventing trespassing on the property of the railroad. The scouts were asked to assist in preventing children from throwing stones at trains. I could find no further information regarding the effectiveness of this outreach.[25]

Kerkam's 1915 Safety First program may have been effective, but it didn't sit well with many people. Suddenly, the tired businessman on his way home from work in the city had a new worry. If he dared to cross the railroad tracks while the safety gates were down in his hurry to get home to his wife and supper, he would be arrested and spend the night in jail before being fined one dollar. During the first week of the campaign thirty-two tired businessmen were arrested by Long Island Railroad policemen. Superintendent Kerkam utilized an old city ordinance that prohibited the crossing of railroad tracks when the gates were lowered. Every evening during the week LIRR police officers were stationed at busy crossings to arrest those who ducked under the gates or walked around them. Kerkam's campaign played no favorites either. Three LIRR employees were among those arrested. The LIRR had printed warnings posted at every crossing with the gatemen on duty directed to verbally warn prospective violators before they passed around or under the gate. The only information I could find regarding the duration of this enforcement campaign was that it was scheduled to continue until the public learned not to cross the tracks when the gates were down.[26]

On May 15, 1917 George Mammen was appointed Superintendent of the Long Island Railroad Police Department. I could find no record or information detailing the circumstances of Robert Kerkam's departure.

Mammen was born in New York City in 1866 and began his railroad career in 1882 as a messenger in the accounting department of the Long Island Railroad. He served in various capacities within the accounting department before his appointment as superintendent of police.[27]

In 1917 the war in Europe had emotions in America running high, especially when it came to statements considered anti-American or unpatriotic, even if the statements were made by a usually trusted source. Such was the case for 39-year-old George Feustel, a conductor on the Long Island Railroad for 19-years. While working his assigned train run Feustel said that President Woodrow Wilson and his cabinet should all be "blown to hell!" He also said he had two brothers serving in the U.S. military, and that they both were going to switch over to the German side at the first opportunity, and that he would do the same thing if he was there. Feustel continued to say that the American Army consisted of nothing but tin soldiers who had no chance of defeating the German Army.

Lieutenant Joseph Naudin of the LIRR Police received several complaints from passengers of the conductor's disparaging remarks. When Naudin confronted Feustel he readily admitted making the statements. Naudin arrested Feustel for disorderly conduct in that his statements constituted a breach of the peace. When Feustel was brought before magistrate Doyle in Jamaica, he was surprised to learn of the complaints made by the passengers who he considered his friends. Magistrate Doyle sentenced Feustel to 30-days in jail. I suppose free speech has its limits, especially during wartime.[28]

Former superintendent Kerkam had received criticism when his safety first campaign resulted in numerous working men returning home after work spending the night in jail for the egregious offense of walking around or ducking under the lowered railroad gates at a crossing. Three years later Superintendent Mammen was chastised for the arrest of eleven working men in Ozone Park. The men were carted off to jail as if they were murderers, but what had they done. These reputable men had the audacity to walk along a path on the LIRR embankment between Ozone Park and Woodhaven Junction.

Patrolman John Bradley arrested the men, even though they claimed they had been using the path for years and that there were no signs prohibiting its use, nor had they received any warning.[29]

Some things never change, and an unfortunate reality is that there will always be creeps and perverts walking among us. I can't begin to tell you how may creeps I came in contact with on the NYC subway system during the 1980s. The Long Island Railroad in 1919 was not immune from the presence of perverts. 31-year-old William Cayea, a builder from Woodhaven was arrested by LIRR officer Frank Quayle on the Brooklyn Manor station. Actually, Cayea wasn't on the station, he was under it. The married father of five was found under the station platform where he was plying his trade as a peeping tom as he attempted to obtain a view under female dresses. When Cayea was brought into court, several attendants recognized him as being in jail previously for the exact same offense.[30]

After my career with the new York City Transit Police and NYPD I thought I had encountered just about every weird and kooky situation cops could get themselves involved with, but there was a 1919 incident involving two Long Island Railroad police officers that was a new one on me.

It's common for police work to run in families so there was nothing odd about Coles Carpenter and his son Latting Carpenter both being police officers with the Long Island Railroad. Father and son were out together with their wives on a Saturday night when they became embroiled in a heated argument on Fulton Street in Jamaica. The elder Carpenter accused his son of striking his mother before knocking his son down with a punch. The son recovered and punched his father. A city police officer found the off duty father and son brawling on Fulton Street. Upon learning they were LIRR patrolmen the city officer was willing to send all parties on their way, but Coles Carpenter insisted on pressing charges against his son and Latting wanted to press counter charges against his father. That was the first and only time I ever heard of a case of father and son cops insisting on pressing charges against each other.[31]

Robert Kerkam,
Chief of Long Island Railroad Police.

R. E. KERKAM, SUPT. OF POLICE, OF LONG ISLAND RAILROAD.

Police in Uniform Are in Attendance at 63 Crossings

A QUARTET OF TRAFFIC OFFICERS

POLICEMAN FREDERICK DE BOSCHE.

1920 – 1949:

The Roaring Twenties was a time of great change in America, but theft of railroad freight continued to be a problem for rail lines across the country, including the Long Island Railroad. In June of 1920 Superintendent Mammen was able to puff his chest and announce what he referred to as the biggest police cleanup on the LIRR in twenty-five years. Working in cooperation with the New York City Police Detective Bureau, the Long Island Railroad Police arrested six men for looting LIRR freight trains and recovered $14,000 worth of loot. Mammen also provided a warning to other looters when he swore to run down and arrest every person involved with freight thefts, even those dating back years.[32]

Superintendent Mammen also experienced success in creating the "Platform Squad." In the Spring of 1920 the growth of travel on the Long Island Railroad, with the resultant congestion on the Jamaica station platforms, had reached such proportions that a uniformed squad of police officers was created to address the issue. The wisdom of the move was immediately apparent in the maintenance of order, prevention of congestion, and the rapid, harmonious handling of the thousands of commuters on the platforms. Sometimes, arrests were a necessary remedy, but the work of the platform squad represented a real growth is the safe environment of the station.[33]

Superintendent Mammen's chest deflated along with his bluster when he became involved with his own problems. One of the first Long Island Railroad stations was Union Course, which serviced the racetrack which was located in what is now Woodhaven, Queens. In 1923 there was a terrible accident at the crossing where a fire truck was hit by a train resulting in the death of three firemen.

The District Attorney of Queens, Dana Wallace, concluded that gross negligence was the cause of the accident, and he ordered the arrest of two LIRR employees – Robert Brinkley, the tower man, and Joseph Rubin, the crossing watchman.

Wallace said it was almost incredible to think that the railroad would place either of these men at such a dangerous crossing. Rubin had been on his job just one day and said he had never directed traffic before or received any formal training. Brinkley said he did not know whether the bells to lift the crossing gate had sounded in his tower, but he insisted that Rubin gave him a signal to raise the gates. Rubin said he did not hear a warning bell, but he admitted signaling to Brinkley to raise the gates.

Rubin and Brinkley tried to shift the blame to the train engineer, but the District Attorney would have none of it. He indicted the two LIRR employees for manslaughter and focused on how the LIRR could place such incompetent personnel at such as dangerous crossing. He determined that the LIRR was negligent in placing Brinkley and Rubin at the Union Course crossing without the proper training and experience and subsequently indicted C. Dwight Baker, the General Superintendent of the Long Island Railroad, and George Mammen, the Superintendent of Long Island Railroad Police.[34]

The indictments against Baker and Mammen were dismissed a year later, but the stress of the arrest and possible trial had to have weighed heavily on Mammen's ability to run the police department, especially when it happened again.[35]

On January 27, 1924, a married couple who resided in Elmhurst was crossing that tracks near the Laurel Hill station in Queens when their automobile was struck by a speeding LIRR train. The couple were killed in the crash.

The crossing watchman was not on his post at the time of the crash and was arrested for manslaughter. The investigation revealed that the gates were frozen in the up position, and that the freezing gates were a common problem during the cold weather. As in the previous case, the Queens District Attorney believed the LIRR may be criminally liable for allowing the dangerous condition to exist. The DA considered indicting Baker and Mammen for manslaughter, but I could find no record of an indictment, leading me to believe that he ultimately decided against the indictments.[36]

Based on the preceding stories it may seem that there was little detail to safety taken at the LIRR crossings – but that was not true. The watchmen assigned to these crossings were considered the backbone of the protection in these areas, and it was their sole interest and duty too protect lives and property at their assigned crossing. While much was left to their discretion in handling unusual conditions that arose, all of their regular duties and rules for conduct were carefully defined in a set of instructions that were posted prominently in each watchman's shanty.

The equipment issued at each crossing for use by the watchman consisted of a book of rules, a hand "stop" disc, two red flags properly mounted on staffs, one white lantern, two red lanterns, several fusees, and one pair of gate lamps for each set of gates. The book of rules covered the used of this equipment.

At very busy crossings a trafficman was sometimes assigned to assist the watchman. The normal position of the trafficman was in the center of the crossing, keeping a lookout in all directions. When a train approached, he blew one blast on a whistle as a signal for the watchman to lower the crossing gates. After the train had passed, he blew two blasts on the whistle as a signal for the watchman to raise the gates.[37]

Just because the failure of watchmen to perform their duties at crossings received major press coverage, it should not be overlooked that the overwhelming majority of these watchmen performed their duties correctly, and sometimes heroically.

Harrison Borah was a very genial man who was posted as a watchman at the Tulip Avenue crossing in Floral Park. He never considered himself a hero, but it was his quick wit and fearlessness that saved the life of an elderly woman one Sunday evening. Mr. Borah had lowered the gates for a westbound express train and had stepped on the tracks to locate a switch engine that was backing along the tracks near the Plainfield Avenue freight station. Suddenly, he observed a woman walking down the westbound track ahead of the express. The engineer saw her and blew his whistle, but she did not react to the warning. Mr. Borah expected the woman to step aside when she reached the crossing, but instead she passed him and continued until she reached the fence that separated the east and westbound tracks. Here, she was hemmed in with nowhere to go as the express train bore down on her. Borah quickly realized her predicament and rushed to her. He held the women in his arms and pressed himself and the woman up against the fence until the train had passed.[38]

Another example of modesty and attention to duty could be found in crossing watchman Angelo Barone. Barone's regular post was the Cornaga Avenue crossing in Far Rockaway. No one would ever have known about his heroic action if not for a letter received from a commuter by Superintendent Mammen. The letter very simply stated that on Sunday afternoon the crossing guard at the Cornaga Avenue crossing had saved a young child's life and nearly lost his own in the process. Superintendent Mammen immediately conducted an investigation, and Barone reluctantly admitted to his heroism.

Barone said that at about 5:30 PM on July 20, 1924, the gates at the Cornaga Avenue crossing had been lowered for east and westbound trolley cars. He said that several automobiles were stopped on both the north and south sides of the crossing, and on the south side of the crossing a man and a boy who looked to be about 9-years of age were also waiting. Barone said the eastbound trolley passed and stopped at the platform. At that time, he continued, the man and boy walked around the gate hand in hand. He said the boy appeared to be carrying a box of candy and when they reached the center of the crossing the boy broke away from the man and started running across the tracks and in front of the approaching westbound trolley, which was a special that was not making a station stop. Barone said he ran toward the boy and grabbed him when the trolley was about ten feet away. He said he threw himself and the boy to the north side of the track and barely cleared the passing trolley. Barone said the boy was uninjured except for a slight scratch on one of his legs. Barone received a bruise to his left hip for which he visited Dr. Corvelli in Far Rockaway, and the returned to his post and continued performing his duties.

Sometimes it wasn't a single incident that brought accolades for devotion to duty. In the case of John Monahan it was more than twenty-five years of diligent duty at the same post.

To those who knew him Monahan was better known as the "Hero of Monahan Junction," the LIRR grade crossing of the Montauk and Long Beach Divisions, at Atlantic Avenue. As he reached his 25th anniversary with the LIRR, the prior 21-years had been spent working at that same crossing.

During his time at the crossing Monahan received five citations for saving people's lives at the crossing. There was never a fatality or serious injury while Monahan was on his post. Monahan could not remember the exact number of people he snatched from the path of an oncoming train, and very modestly noted that his actions were all part of being a railroad cop. [39]

Some acts of heroism at a crossing also had their humorous value. One day an artist who contributed to the LIRR Informational Bulletin was waiting for a train at the Valley Stream station. The artist looked to the tracks and noticed a small dog sitting calmly on the eastbound tracks happily yelping at its female owner who was frantically yelling for her dog to get off the tracks. Bearing down from the east in a cloud of dense black smoke was a mammoth locomotive. Also waiting on the platform was LIRR Police Captain Toombs. When the Captain recognized the impending tragedy, he crouched down and like the Pied Piper of Hamlin, calmly emitted such sweet sounds from his lips that so charmed the little dog that he immediately pranced into Toombs' arms.

Captain Toombs turned to the owner and handed the little dog to her, saying, "See, that's the way to do it." [40]

Sometimes, a crossing watchman performed his job well, but still managed to receive complaints. In this case, the complaints were generated by the superintendent of a swanky apartment building near the Jackson and Columbia Street crossing in Hempstead. According to the superintendent the crossing watchman killed time in between trains by playing a fiddle, which highly annoyed the residents of his building. It was unclear whether it was simply the music the residents objected to or the quality of the fiddle playing. [41]

With his indictment problems behind him, Superintendent Mammen was clear to move ahead with advancements to the police force. What he moved into, however, was the Great Train Robbery.

Some of the most famous crimes of the old west were train robberies committed by some of the most famous criminals, like Jesse James and Butch Cassidy's Wild Bunch. Contrary to the methods romanticized by Hollywood, outlaws were never known to jump from horseback onto a moving train. Usually, they boarded the train along with other passengers and waited for a good time to initiate the heist, or they would stop or derail the train and then begin the holdup. Trains carrying a payroll shipment were a major target, even though an expressman guarded these shipments. Bandits often overtook this guard by gunpoint and forced him to open the safe. If he did not have the combination, dynamite was used to blow it up. But over time, railroads wised up. Many added massive, unmovable safes to their trains and often hired armed guards. Some even added cars with armed men and horses who could be deployed to chase down any bandits who robbed the train. By the turn of the 20th century, most of the famous train robbers, including Butch Cassidy, the Sundance Kid, and the other members of the Wild Bunch gang had been captured, killed, or were no longer operating in the United States.

By 1925, train robberies were primarily a memory from America's past. During their history, the Long Island Railroad had never experienced a train robbery, that is until January 13th, 1925.[42]

John Greene had been a mail clerk with the Long Island Railroad for fifteen years. For the last five years he had worked on the Montauk Division on a Patchogue to New York train. It seemed like another normal evening as Greene followed the same routine he had done for the prior five years. Train #71 consisted of a baggage car, mail car, and six passenger coaches. The engineer was E. Dermott and John Barry was the conductor. The train departed Patchogue at 5:04 PM and at 6:30 it pulled into the Bellmore station.

Adjacent to the tracks at the station, the station agent waited at the position where the mail car would stop. John Greene stood in the open door and easily caught the three pouches tossed by the station agent. Greene turned as he tossed the pouches to the side. The train was stopped at Bellmore for no more than thirty seconds and he was already thinking about the four minutes he would have to begin sorting his mail during the trip from Bellmore to Merrick. Suddenly, Greene felt a tug on his belt that contained his holstered 38 caliber Smith & Wesson revolver. A man grabbed the gun and when Green turned, he observed the man pointing the gun directly at his face. The man looked to be about 22-years old and was wearing a dark cap and coat. He also wore a white handkerchief with black dots over the bottom portion of his face. The crook told Green to raise his hands and remain quiet or else he would fill him full of lead and throw him out of the train on his head.

The bandit seemed to know exactly which pouch to take. He took the pouch and motioned for Greene to open the door. The train was traveling at 25 mph and the crook must have realized it was too fast to jump, so he stood at the door while keeping the pistol trained on Greene.

The bandit waited until the train had slowed and was just about to enter the Merrick station before he leaped into the darkness and disappeared. Green rushed to a grocery store and reported the crime.[43]

The day after the robbery, the LIRR tried to distance itself from the crime. George Flatow, the Director of Railroad Publicity explained that the robbery was only indirectly a railroad matter because the mail pouch and mail car were under the custody of the United States Government. Superintendent of Long Island Railroad Police George Mammen said that his railroad police were not supposed to guard mail cars, and that the Government does not request protective aid from him. Mammen said that once the robbery was reported, the Long Island Railroad Police immediately went to work on the case, and that to the best of his knowledge this was the first robbery of its kind on the LIRR.[44]

Immediately after police arrived at the Merrick station, the emptied mail pouch, a registered package containing bluing samples, a small whited dotted handkerchief and a 32-caliber automatic pistol of German make were found near the end of the platform. A police dog from Hempstead was quickly on the scene but lost the scent a few hundred feet from the station.

Both the railroad and county police originally believed the robbery may have been committed by Gerald Chapman. Chapman was known as the "lone mail car robber" and had operated extensively in the Eastern United States. To add credibility to this theory, Chapman fit the description of the robber provided by Greene, and he had recently escaped from the Federal Prison in Atlanta. A conductor also identified a photo of Chapman as a man who had questioned him a week earlier regarding shipments of money on mail trains.[45]

The day after the robbery, two brothers named Esposito were walking along a road in Astoria when a Chrysler Roadster came speeding past them. As the sports car sped by something came flying out the window of the vehicle. They picked up the bag from the side of the road and brought it to the Astoria Police Precinct where it was eventually identified as the bag that had contained the stolen $10,000. A short distance from where the Esposito brothers found the bag, another man picked up a package of letters. The man took the package to a Long Island City Post Office branch where it was found to be the registered letters from the pouch that also contained the money.

More leads began to trickle in. Witnesses stated that for three nights before the robbery, and on the night of the crime, there had been a Chrysler Roadster parked without lights on near the Merrick crossing a few hundred feet from the station at the time the 6:34 train pulled in.[46]

Local and federal law enforcement agencies worked non-stop on the case. For the Long Island Road Police, Lieutenant Frederick Gottlieb, Lieutenant Joseph Naudin, Sergeant Joseph Wogan, and Patrolmen Lincoln Ross, Oscar Liles, and George Davis worked tirelessly on the case.

The big break in the case came primarily from the work of one cop. During the three-day manhunt the crook had rested in perfect security. After all, the police were on the trail of Gerald Chapman as the train robber, leaving the real crook in the clear.

It was Lester Chadwick, a Captain with the Village of Lynbrook Police Department who was chiefly responsible for solving the robbery. When Chadwick learned of the leads involving a Chrysler Roadster he decided it would be a good idea to check up on people in his town who owned sports cars. He visited the district sales agency and learned that John Cadoo had recently purchased a Chrysler Roadster on the partial payment plan. When Chadwick went to question Cadoo, he noticed that Cadoo had a cut over his eye.

Chadwick returned to his headquarters, but he realized that the cut over the eye of one of the few owners of a Roadster in the area was worthy of further investigation. At 10 PM Chadwick directed two of his police officers, Harold King and Harold Sinclair, to bring Cadoo to the station house for further questioning.

The policemen rapped on the door of the Cadoo apartment and were greeted by the soft voice of Cadoo's wife behind the locked door asking what they wanted. When the cops told her they wanted to talk to Cadoo they could hear whispering behind the door. A minute later the woman whispered that her husband was not at home and would be out all night.

The two policemen reported back to Captain Chadwick, who promptly contacted the federal authorities. Postal Inspectors and local police descended on Cadoo's home. While the postal inspectors questioned Cadoo, the police searched the house and garage. In the back of the car, they found a black handbag which contained all but $114.00 of the stolen money. When confronted with the evidence Cadoo broke down and admitted that he was the train robber.[47]

22-year-old John W. Cadoo told the authorities he had acted alone, and that he committed the crime so that he could have money to support his 17-year-old wife. He denied vigorously that he had been tipped off that the money was to be shipped. He said that he knew shipments were made regularly and that he just took a chance.

For four years Cadoo was employed as a clerk in the main post office in Manhattan. Later, he was transferred to Lynbrook, where he worked until he resigned about a month before the robbery. Since then, he drifted from job to job. In one short month Cadoo worked as a hosiery salesman, a real estate promoter, and a furniture salesman. Cadoo said he needed the money and that it looked easy to rob a mail car.

Cadoo conceived the idea of the robbery about ten days before the heist but did not actually work out the details until a couple of days before the robbery. He actually started to commit the crime a day earlier but could complete the job. He had parked his Roadster near the Hewlitt Avenue crossing and walked back to the Merrick station.

When the 6:30 train arrived, he walked down the platform and waited for a chance to jump aboard the mail car as the train pulled out of the station. The train picked up speed too quickly, however, and he aborted his plan to attempt the leap.

The next day Cadoo was back in the same position. He stood on the platform as the train pulled into the Merrick station. He watched the station agent throw the bags to Greene. He saw Greene lift one of the bags and turn his back to the door. This was the chance he was waiting for. Cadoo quickly adjusted his mask and swung up on the iron rung and into the open door. While Greene's back was still turned Cadoo grabbed the pistol from Greene's belt. Cadoo commented that getting the drop on Greene was very easy, as the mail clerk showed no fight at all. He grabbed the pouch that he believed held money and forced Greene to back into a corner while he waited for the train to approach Merrick. As the train slowed down at the Hewlitt crossing, a moment before the train pulled into the Merrick station, Cadoo jumped. Even though the train had slowed considerably, he still misjudged the speed causing him to slip on the insecure footing of the snow and ice. Cadoo tumbled over on his side and slid along over the snow. The package of money went flying in one direction, the pistol he carried in another direction.

As quickly as he could, Cadoo regained his footing and picked up the money. He was still groggy as he ran to his parked car. Cadoo reiterated that he committed the crime because he was newly married and wanted his wife to believe he had made good.[48]

Cadoo said the robbery had actually provided several thrills for him. The greatest of these was when he read in the newspapers that Gerald Chapman was suspected of committing the crime.[49]

John Cadoo was sentenced to 25-years in prison. There was a outcry of public support for Cadoo due to the harsh nature of his sentence. A petition addressed to President Calvin Coolidge requesting for Cadoo's release received hundreds of signatures from residents of Lynbrook.[50]

On December 5, 1928 John Cadoo's sentence was commuted to fifteen years. I could find no record of how long he actually served in prison.[51]

John Cadoo died in April 1965 at the age of 64. He is buried in Green-Wood Cemetery in Brooklyn.[52]

After Cadoo was sentenced to prison the Supervisory Postal Inspector sent a letter to LIRR Police Superintendent George Mammen thanking the work of the Long Island Railroad Police in the capture of John Cadoo.

In 1928 The Pennsylvania Railroad and Long Island Railroad consolidated into the New York Zone. At that time, George Mammen was appointed a special agent with the Pennsylvania Railroad's Police Department in New York City. Although it doesn't sound like it, apparently, the move from Superintendent of the Long Island Railroad Police to the special agent position was a promotion. Mammen remained as a special agent for three years before retiring at the age of 65 after completing fifty years with the railroad.[53]

Superintendent Mammen had issues over the years with accidents at crossings, facing indictments personally on two occasions for alleged negligence on his part. It was somewhat ironic that just as he was stepping down from his position as superintendent of the LIRR police, he received a silver loving cup as evidence of the police department compiling the best safety record in the railroad during 1927. In his presentation address, Safety Supervisor Thomas Brennan cited the good work the police department had done in curtailing accidents, particularly at grade crossings.

Mammen was likely thinking of the problems he experienced with crossing accidents when he called attention to the great problems his men had to face at grade crossings.[54]

The next chief to take the helm of the LIRR Police Department was Laurance Ballou. Ballou, who served in the Federal Secret Service during World War I, entered the LIRR's employ in 1904 as a ticket clerk at Manhattan Beach. He was promoted to station agent at Lynbrook, and from there he was sent to the Pennsylvania Railroad as a fireman, and then a towerman. His first experience as a railroad detective was in the Pennsylvania coal fields, where it was reported that his fairness, courage and powerful physique won respect among the miners. From 1917 to 1922 Ballou was in the Secret Service, from which he returned to the LIRR as an assistant Chief Clerk in the Police Department with the rank of lieutenant. He was promoted to Captain in 1927 and the following year he was placed in charge of the department.[55]

It wasn't long before Chief Ballou had to deal with the political fallout from a theft ring. The politics did not involve the crime, but instead was all about the location of the crime. In 1929 the Borough Hall of Queens was a peculiarly isolated building that rose six stories on a small triangle of ground that was completely surrounded by vast railroad yards. The view from the window of the Borough President's office commanded a wide swath of territory in Long Island City and a huge portion of the railroad yards. Unfortunately, the most familiar sight for the Borough President had become the almost daily thefts of coal from the railroad yards by a gang of youths. The scheme first came to the Borough President's attention as he peered out his window at a boy of about 9-years of age standing on the viaduct that crossed all the railroad yards at Van Alst Avenue. The boy stood, keen eyed and silent, watching the tracks below. He spoke to no one and moved away if anyone walked near him. The Borough President initially believed the young fellow was simply fascinated by the movement of the trains in the yard. But as days passed and the sightings of the boy continued, he noticed the boy making odd motions with his arms. The Borough President had not been watching a boy in love with trains. He was watching the lookout for a gang of coal thieves.

The Borough President was irate at the brazen criminal activity taking place right outside his window. In a conference with newspaper reporters, he demanded that the LIRR do something to stop the thefts. One of the reporters at the conference found one of the young thieves and got the lad to agree to an interview over a meal at a diner.

The youth said he was fourteen years old and that the younger boys in the gang worked as the lookouts. He said that the boy the Borough President had seen on the viaduct was a lookout, but that there was another lookout on an embankment on Hunters Point Avenue. The young thief said that his gang usually operated in the yards in teams of two or three as they moved among the strings of freight cars, crawling under them and dodging out of sight at the approach of a switchman or a railroad cop. The youth explained that the lookouts were supposed to look closely for the railroad cops because they were a "hard boiled lot," who didn't hesitate to use a club or fist. He said the railroad cops were not as kind-hearted as the blue-coated, silver badged policemen of the city. The boy said the city blue coats learned their professions guarding school crossings and were more sympathetic with the youngsters. The boy stopped and took a deep breath before claiming that the railroad cops were taught their jobs by bouncing hoboes and that they were taught to be tough, rough, and quick to take action. The lad went on to say that the railroad cops just didn't like kids because to a railroad cop, kids meant mischief.

The thief said that when the gang got down to work they would scoot around the tracks picking up pieces of coal that had rolled from locomotive tenders or coal cars. He said that some hoboes had a great scheme going where they would stand next to the tracks and when the train came by, they would yell and make faces at the fireman, who would get so upset that he would hurl pieces of coal at them. The boy said it was a good racket, but it would not work in the yards. He said it took a couple of hours of rapid, non-stop coal collection to fill three fifty-pound sacks.

The reporter took note of the heavy gloves the youth had with him and inquired as to their purpose. The lad said that the gloves served an important purpose. If they were seen by a railroad cop in the middle of the coal collection, they had numerous places in the yards they could quickly stash their coal sacks. Besides stashing the coal, the boy emphasized that the gloves also had to be stashed. He said when the cop caught up to him and asked what he was doing, the cop was eventually going to demand to see his hands and evidence that coal had been handled. Instead, the boy was able to display completely clean hands to the confused, irritated cop who consoled himself by kicking the kids out of the yard. The youth said it was bad that they would lose their haul of coal, but it was much better than taking a licking from the cop before being sent to jail.

When they weren't interrupted by the railroad cops the boy said the haul of coal was loaded onto a home-made wagon made from an old baby carriage and wheeled out of the yard. The young man would not reveal what the gang did with the coal.

The day after the interview there was an interesting and somewhat humorous event that took place outside the doors of Borough Hall. The gang had completed a haul and were moving the coal-filled wagon up Hunter's Point Avenue. Automobile traffic was heavy and while two of the gang served as a rear guard to keep watch for cops coming up from behind them, the other two maneuvered the wagon through traffic. Directly in front of the entrance to Borough Hall it happened. One of the bags of coal came open and as the wagon had to dodge an automobile, before the youths could steady the wagon all the coal had spilled out of the bag and onto the pavement.

For a moment the gang debated uneasily what to do. One little fellow started scooping up some of the coal in his cap while another tried to put some of the pieces back in the bag. With so many witnesses watching, after a few minutes the gang fled, leaving a substantial pile of coal in the street. Throughout the day the stolen coal was crushed under the tires of passing automobiles, some of them the huge shiny cars of officials working inside Borough Hall.[56]

Police Departments always take pride when an officer's achievement makes him stand out among other police departments. Such was the case for Long Island Railroad Police Officer Lincoln Ross in 1929. During this era New York State ran a training school for police officers to ensure that officers around the state received proper police training. Periodically, officers from Nassau and Suffolk Counties, as well as the LIRR Police would be invited to send officers to the ten-lesson course in Mineola. More than 600 officers attended the session in 1929, and LIRR officer Ross ranked highest in the class by scoring a 96% on the final examination.[57]

Up to that point Ross's career had been somewhat of a roller coaster. Four years earlier he had been embroiled in the Queens crossing accident that killed a married couple. Ross was indicted for manslaughter along with superintendent of police Mammen because it was alleged that Ross had received a phone call notifying him that the gates were frozen in the up position and took no action to correct the condition. As with Mammen, the indictment against Ross was dropped and he was able to continue his career.[58]

In 1926 it was LIRR Detective Ross who broke up a ring of young thieves stealing cigarettes from freight cars in the Glendale Yard.[59] Then it was Sergeant Ross who solved the case of a $632 robbery of a collection in the Dunton Yard. Along with detectives from the Richmond Hill city precinct, Ross arrested a former freight conductor and an ex-New York City cop for the crime. William Macken had been dismissed from the city police department a year earlier for shooting up a Jamaica Cabaret. In his confession he cited "hard times" as the motive for his crime.[60]

Four years after his academic achievement, in 1933 Sergeant Lincoln Ross broke up the notorious "Whistle Gang." For months engineers been shocked when they attempted to blow their whistles and heard nothing but silence. Further inspection would always reveal a good reason for the silence. The 8-pound brass whistle was gone. Ross rounded up three boys in the darkness of the yard just west of the Jamaica station and recovered three whistles.[61]

A recurring issue for all the LIRR police chiefs were the numerous issues at the crossings. Chief Ballou was not exempt from the crossing concerns, although he did manage to avoid indictment during his tenure.

Sometimes the problems at a crossing were not caused by an on duty officer not doing his job. On one occasion it was an on duty officer who thought he was above the law that was the issue. At approximately 4 AM on January 29, 1929, LIRR crossing watchman George Young was on his post at the Wellwood Avenue crossing in Lindenhurst. The gates were down as a train had just pulled into the station when a police car driven by Amityville Police Officer Irvin Chichester pulled up to the gate. Officer Chichester demanded that Young raise the gate for him, but Young said he would have to wait until the train pulled out of the station. Chichester then accelerated and crashed through the lowered gate. Naturally, Chichester made no report of the incident but Young reported it to his superiors in the LIRR. When Amityville police officials questioned Chichester he had no excuse for crashing through the gate. The officials also wanted to know what Chichester was doing outside of Amityville to which he explained that he was following a vehicle that he feared may run out of gas. Chichester probably would have been better off saying he had no excuse for being outside of Amityville.[62]

In 1931 a Mineola man was killed when a train crashed into his vehicle at the Roslyn Road crossing. The gate had been down and when the vehicle approached crossing watchman Cyril Pasco inexplicitly raised the gate just as the train was about to roar past.[63] In 1932 six crossing watchmen assigned to crossings in the Rockaways were arrested for the misdemeanor of being absent from their posts while on duty. Two of the six were additionally charged with grand larceny in connection with the theft of money from telephone coin boxes and automatic vending machines in the Rockaway LIRR station.[64]

I know there is no criminal charge of stupidity in the first degree, but some stories just beg for this addition to the Penal law. In 1929 two New York State Troopers working in Bayshore received a call from an anonymous source that police better get to the LIRR West Islip Yard quickly before a tragedy occurred. Troopers Giasheen and Martin hurried to the scene to find that a crew of LIRR workers – drunk LIRR workers – were taking an afternoon nap. It wasn't bad enough that the crew was drunk and sleeping when they were supposed to be working. This crew used as a pillow the wooden guard of the electrified third rail. They peacefully snored while their heads rested inches away from electrocution. The troopers piled them all into their car and brought them before a judge, where they were fined $10 each for public intoxication.[65]

1931 records released by the LIRR reflected that 1,777 people were arrested for twenty different illegal acts committed against LIRR people and property. In 1,627 of these cases convictions were obtained. The majority of the arrests were for juvenile delinquency and trespassing. Of the 773 cases in which children were arrested many involved acts that might have caused hundreds of railroad patrons to lose their lives or become seriously injured. For example, several boys were apprehended removing jumper wires from rails and switches, thereby opening up the possibility of a train wreck. Some boys were caught shooting air rifles and throwing stones at signals and passing trains. Others were discovered breaking into freight houses, removing seals and pilfering valuable shipments from freight cars in transit.

754 individuals, mostly boys and girls of school age, were arrested for trespassing on railroad property.

Other arrests included:

• Disorderly conduct on trains and stations 95

- Larceny 71
- Intoxication 24
- Vagrancy 10
- Assault 9
- Motor vehicle violation 8
- Burglary 7
- Malicious mischief 7
- Jumping through car windows at terminals 5
- Illegal car riding 3
- Taxicab violations 3
- Unlawful entry 2
- Discharging firearms 1
- Depositing rubbish on railroad property 1
- Indecent exposure 1
- Receiving stolen goods 1
- Sending threatening letter 1
- Child running away from home 1 [66]

In 1941 the country's focus shifted to World War II. LIRR Police Chief Ballou was uniquely qualified to see the LIRR Police Department through the war years. The chief's police officers were on duty 24-hours a day - at night when the troop trains rolled and during the day when commuter expresses sped toward the city. Unobserved by the public at large, seasoned railroad detectives efficiently covered vital locations, always alert for disorder, violence, and the greatest wartime menace - sabotage. In uniform and plainclothes LIRR police patrolled teeming yards where war supplies were loaded, humming shops where heavily burdened rolling stock was kept in repair, and busy platforms, stations and terminals thronged with wartime crowds. By this time all LIRR officers were commissioned as New York State peace officers, and they worked closely with city, state, and county police, as well as the FBI, Army and Navy Intelligence, and the Coast Guard. Chief

Ballou's service during World War I with the Federal Secret Service was particularly valuable during the years of World War II.

Chief Ballou wasn't always involved with thwarting attempts at sabotage and espionage, as he still managed to find some leisure time. Ballou was the leader of the Nassau County Police Glee Club, and his choir performed regularly at events during the war years.[67]

ANGELO BARONE

Watchman who saved a child at a crossing

The hero of Monahan Junction

CHIEF OF LONG ISLAND RAILROAD POLICE

Laurance Ballou

HARRISON BORAH

Watchman who saved elderly woman at crossing

CLEAR
THAT
TRACK
AHEAD!
HERE Boy!
HeRe Boy
HEY!!
I CAPT. TOOMBS   II MISS DISTRESS

Artist depiction of Captain Toombs' "heroic" dog-saving.

The Platform Squad

Loyal to Bandit

Wife of train robber John Cadoo

SERGEANT JOSEPH L. WOGAN

One of the LIRR officers who worked on the "Great Train Robbery"

1950 – 1979:

On February 17,1950, 55-year-old Jacob Kiefer was doing what he had done for the prior 27-years. He was at the controls of eastbound Babylon bound Long Island Railroad train #78 as it sped through the Nassau County village of Rockville Centre. At the time, the Montauk Branch was undergoing a program to eliminate grade crossings, where the roadway and track intersected at the same elevation. A new elevated viaduct was being constructed just north of the original at-grade railroad line's right-of-way. As a result, the original line's right-of-way narrowed to one gauntlet track shared by both westbound and eastbound trains for about 2 miles located partly on a curve. At the gauntlet track, the two tracks ran parallel on a single track bed. The pairs of tracks overlapped, so only one pair of rails were able to be used at a time. There was a signal west of Banks Avenue for eastbound trains, and train traffic movements into the gauntlet track were controlled by a dispatcher at Rockville Centre station. Everything was normal for the engineer until the scene went dark.

In retrospect, Jacob Kiefer wished the scene had remained black. It would have spared him the unspeakable horror of what had just occurred. A red signal had illuminated to stop Kiefer's eastbound train to allow a westbound train to pass first on the gauntlet track. The eastbound train blew through the red signal and the head on collision occurred at 10:43 PM.

First responders came from all over the region. Every firefighter and police officer in Lynbrook and Rockville Centre was summoned to the site of the crash. Two hours after the collision, only six bodies had been extracted from the wreckage, and many of the injured were still trapped. To prevent rescue workers from being electrocuted, the LIRR cut power to the gauntlet track's third rails after receiving reports of the crash. In total, 250 doctors and 450 firefighters and LIRR emergency workers responded to the crash, along with numerous volunteers. The injured were transported to nearby hospitals such as South Nassau Community Hospital, which became overcrowded as a result.

Because many movie theaters were playing films at the time of the crash, there were thousands of people in the vicinity. As these films concluded, many of these moviegoers and others went to see the crash. Police officers estimated that by one hour after the crash, there were 30,000 people near the wreck, many of whom attempted to observe from several miles away.

The next information Jacob Kiefer could process was that thirty-two people were dead and another hundred injured and he was under arrest for manslaughter with no explanation for what had happened. Months later Kiefer was acquitted of the manslaughter charges when a jury believed his claim that blood pressure medication had caused him to black out just as the red signal came into view.

The terrible tragedy that occurred in Rockville Centre was not the primary reason I included the story in this book. After his arraignment for manslaughter $10,000 bail was set. The bail was paid by John C. Valick. What I found intriguing about this bail transaction was that Valick was an employee of the LIRR, and not just any employee. Valick was the Superintendent of the Long Island Railroad Police Department. Why would the chief of police be posting the bail for an employee charged with manslaughter? I don't know. But what I also didn't know was exactly when Valick had become head of this police department. This record of him posting the bail in February of 1950 was the first record I could find that listed him as chief of the LIRR police. And what became of Laurance Ballou? Perhaps it is a testament to my lack of research skills, but I could find no record or reference to his descent from the throne of the police department. I found one 1950 newspaper article about Ballou's son. The story mentioned that his father had been the head of the LIRR police until his death two years earlier. Again, my research skills came up short when I failed to locate an obituary for Laurance Ballou. I would have to settle at saying that Ballou had passed away sometime in 1948 and John Valick became chief of the department sometime thereafter. But wait a minute! Remember that Ballou had been the leader of the police glee club. I discovered an article from the middle of 1949 lauding his performance as a solo baritone. Oh well, in any event, John C. Valick was the next chief of the Long Island Railroad Police Department.[68]

Less than a year later the LIRR experienced what is still the worst crash in its history in an accident that became known as the Richmond Hill Disaster. During the evening rush hour on November 22, 1950, two trains collided between the Kew Gardens and Jamaica stations killing 78 people and inuring363.

An eastbound Hempstead-bound train carrying about one thousand passengers experienced brake problems just after the train passed Kew Gardens. The engineer had applied the brakes to reduce speed in response to a "go slow" signal, but once engaged the brakes would not release, resulting in the train coming to a halt. While the engineer tried to fix the problem the brakeman, traveling in the rear car, got out and held a red lantern to warn any trains following. He then heard the traction motors power, and believing that the brakes were now working, he turned off the lantern and re-boarded the train even though he had not received a signal from the train's whistle to return to the train. The brakes were still locked, and the train remained stationery on the tracks with no protection to the rear.

A few minutes later an eastbound Babylon train came around the bend 4,600 feet behind the Hempstead train. It slowed to 15 mph in response to a "go slow" signal indicating congestion ahead. The engineer than saw the next signal beyond the stopped train, which showed "all clear." Thinking the all clear signal applied to him, the engineer accelerated to 35 mph and slammed into the rear of the Babylon train.

In the aftermath of the crash, all of the police detectives on duty in Queens were summoned to the site, as were 200 physicians coming from every hospital in the borough. Police and fire personnel cut through the wreckage with torches and used ladders to allow doctors and nurses to provide medical aid for those trapped inside. Emergency responders were also summoned from other boroughs. It was more than five hours before the last people still alive were removed from the wreckage.

Although it pales in comparison to the two crashes in 1950, vandalism was still a huge problem for the railroad, not only in terms of financial losses, but also for the potential of another crash being caused by these criminal acts.

For example, in 1950 a 17-year-old girl and four teenage boys were arrested by LIRR police officers on felony charges of damaging signal equipment. The teens were nabbed after damaging signals near the Brooklyn Manor station in Woodhaven by pelting the signal with rocks.[69]

Even though technology continued to advance at a rapid pace, some challenges for the LIRR police remained the same. Trespassing and vandalism in train yards continued to be a problem during the decade of the 1950s, sometimes with deadly results. Many did not understand the 1952 decision the railroad made to remove watchmen from some yards.

The LIRR had been ordered by the Public Service Commission in 1947 to keep watchmen in the East New York, Pitkin Avenue, New Lots, and Parkville Avenue yards. The order was given after several incidents where youngsters playing in the yards were electrocuted. The PSC said at that time that even though trespassing and vandalism were to be deplored, the railroad had an obligation through the watchmen guards to protect adventurous youths, lured by the fascination of trains, from themselves.

In allowing the LIRR to remove the guards the PSC required the railroad to close and securely lock gates to the yards at the close of business each day. Additionally, the movement of cars in the Pitkin and

New Lots yards were restricted to hours when the gates were locked. Furthermore, all trains had to come to a stop before entering yards and the LIRR police had to patrol the yards at various times during the day and night.[70]

The decision to remove the guards was odd considering the LIRR was the subject of. $250,000 lawsuit at the time. A nine-year old boy had lost both legs when he was electrocuted while playing near the Bay Ridge cut. The boy testified that he and his friends had played on the railroad property for a few years, even building a clubhouse near the location he was electrocuted, and the LIRR police never chased them away or dismantled their clubhouse during all that time.[71]

Probably the most serious form of vandalism the LIRR police had to contend with were acts that could lead to a derailment. It didn't take much planning or ingenuity to potentially cause a disaster. For example, in 1953 a 15-year-old boy tried three times to derail an LIRR train before he was finally caught. On each occasion the boy placed a box used for carrying milk bottles on the rails in the vicinity of the Queens Village station. The box was filled with ballast and splintered when it was struck by a westbound train causing no damage to the train. In his second attempt in the same area, railroad workers found the box and removed it from the tracks. Because the boy stayed in the same area, the LIRR Police were waiting as he attempted to place a third box on the tracks and took him into custody.[72]

Wrapped around the crime, vandalism, and accidents on the system, the LIRR police also had to deal with passengers every day. Dealing with an irate passenger who believed he was being wronged was always a pleasant experience for a cop. I cite the 1953 case of "Mr. X" because besides fitting the mold of the irate commuter, I also learned something that I didn't know about the LIRR during that era.

After a long day at work Mr. X boarded the 5:01 train to Long Beach at Penn Station as he did every workday. He settled into a seat and tried to get comfortable for his trip to Long Beach. As the train and its one thousand passengers emerged into the daylight of Queens, conductor F.J. Coyle was moving through the cars checking tickets. Mr. X presented his monthly commutation ticket, but Coyle did not continue up the aisle. Instead, he turned and addressed Mr. X., noting that his ticket was improper. Mr. X had a few choice words for the conductor which translated into his request for an explanation. The conductor's explanation was the area where I learned something. Coyle said that for the monthly commutation ticket to be valid Mr. X had to affix his photograph and signature on the ticket after the first six rides.

Mr. X was having none of it, stating indignantly, "I've got my ticket – I don't need a passport to get to Long Beach."

The conductor only added fuel to Mr. X's fire when he told him that since the photo and signature were missing, he would have to pay cash. The dispute escalated causing Coyle to make an unscheduled stop at Kew Gardens to call for police. In the meantime, eleven other trains were now delayed behind the 5:01 to Long Beach.

When the train pulled into Jamaica, LIRR police officers directed Mr. X to pay or get off. He refused both options. Time passed and finally other passengers took up a collection to pay Mr. X's fare, With the train moving again the drama was far from over. Angry passengers told Coyle exactly what they thought of the LIRR while others jumped to the beleaguered conductor's defense. Coyle decided he needed help, so he yanked the emergency cord which stopped the train at Laurelton, another unscheduled stop. Tempers and the temperature inside the train had risen prompting Coyle to open the train doors while waiting for police assistance. About ten minutes later when LIRR police arrived, Mr. X could not be found. Someone said they saw him walk out an open-door muttering complaints about the railroad. He was never seen again.[73]

The arrival of the 1960s found vandalism and juvenile delinquency still top priorities for the Long Island Railroad Police Department. In 1960 Chief Valick announced a plan to combat the problems with much flare and fanfare. Valick announced that his department would sport brand new uniforms in implementing his new "hit-em-by-surprise" campaign to fight vandalism. Under the plan the LIRR police force would scrap its traditional system of having patrolmen cover fixed routes in favor of a fully flexible setup in which there were no predetermined assignments until the men began their daily tours of duty. In theory, this would make it impossible for thieves or vandals to study the patterns of patrols and time their activities when police weren't present. This new system was adopted at a full dress review of the LIRR police force outside the LIRR's Jamaica headquarters.

The police donned their new military style uniforms for the occasion, and were reviewed by top officials from the FBI, NYS Police, and the Nassau and Suffolk Police Departments. The new uniforms were pattered closely after those worn by the New York State Police. They were a lighter shade of blue than traditionally seen in the New York area. They had single breasted jackets with a full military cut, set off by black Sam Browne belts, permitting guns to be carried outside, rather than inside the jackets Chief Valick said the new no-fixed route patrol system, in addition to providing an element of surprise, would permit the LIRR Police Department to concentrate its forces at any point where additional strength would be required to meet an outbreak of vandalism. This reorganization also featured the creation of a plainclothes investigative squad, which operated directly out of Chief Valick's office, which worked closely with detective squads and the FBI on follow up details, leaving other railroad police more time for patrol duty.[74]

As I continue to the next story in the 1960's I have to first recap a small tidbit about the complicated nature of the history of the Long Island Railroad. As mentioned in the introduction, there was a time that the LIRR was owned by the Pennsylvania Railroad. Ever since latter part of the 19th century the LIRR began planning how to establish direct access into Manhattan. The Pennsylvania Railroad simultaneously began planning access across the Hudson River into Manhattan. The Pennsylvania Railroad began construction of a Manhattan terminal which was to become Penn Station, and LIRR President William H. Baldwin Jr. started negotiating in 1900 to enter Penn Station. That same year the Pennsylvania Railroad paid $6 million for a controlling interest in the LIRR. The LIRR remained under Pennsy ownership (or at least some affiliation) until the Metropolitan Transportation Authority took control of the LIRR in 1966. So, in 1962, the LIRR was still associated with the Pennsylvania Railroad and is rationale for this longwinded explanation and the next story.

In 1962 the people who passed through Penn Station each day were unaware they were being watched by the long telescope of a police chief, who stood like a sea captain in his upper deck office as he squinted down at the currents of commuters flowing across the concourse. Usually, Chief Frank J. Holslag, of the Pennsylvania Railroad Police, tried to focus his telescope on purse snatchers, baggage thieves or panhandlers who sometimes lingered around the benches or ticket windows. In 1961 there were 1,598 arrests for various kinds of thievery and loitering in Penn Station. When Chief Holslag spotted a suspect in his lens – the telescope was so powerful he could read a newspaper from 300 feet away – he would press his office intercom to alert a uniformed policeman on the concourse floor below. The uniformed man would then give a signal to a plainclothesman who would move in close to the suspect to observe the crime. When the evidence was obtained the plainclothesman would signal back to the uniformed cop who would make the arrest. The chief's people watching skills brought him into long range intimacy with numerous character and connivers. For example, there were "Frenchy" and the "Cisco Kid," two baggage hustlers who tried to take trade away from the Red Caps and who were never discouraged by numerous arrests.

There were assorted longtime pickpockets, and also "switch key artists," aggregable thieves who kept many locker keys in their pockets, and after helping elderly people hoist luggage into lockers, they would switch the keys and give the key that didn't fit to the elderly person. Later, the thief would return and open the locker with the real key, removing any valuables from the locker.

As of 1962 Chief Holslag had been at Penn Station for nine years. He had only been to the theatre twice during that time period, and whenever his wife wanted to go to a show, he would say, "You wanna see a show? Just come on down here. This is the best show in town." [75]

Economic strife punctuated the decade of the 1970s. US economic stagnation hit New York City particularly hard, amplified by a large movement of middle-class residents to the suburbs, which drained the city of tax revenue. New York City was on the brink of bankruptcy.

On June 30, 1975 the city laid off an initial 15,000 workers, including 3,000 cops and 1,600 firefighters – 20% of the city's entire force. Some 26 fire companies were simply disbanded. By September, 45,000 workers had been laid off. The Transit Authority followed suit and laid off thousands of transit workers, including transit police officers. Since the 3,000-man Transit Police Department was about one tenth the size of the NYPD, 300 transit police officers were proportionately laid off. The economic avalanche quickly blanketed the LIRR police resulting in twenty LIRR officers being laid off.

In December of 1975 LIRR cops staged a rally outside the Jamaica station to protests the layoffs. The LIRR Police Department was already at a low manpower level, as it was noted that the twenty were laid off from a department of 144 officers.

Ken McFeeley, president of the NYPD Patrolmen's Benevolent Association addressed the LIRR cops and told them that the target of their vengeance would be to oust every Assemblyman, every Congressman and every politician who stood against the police.

An advantage that the twenty laid off patrolmen shared with the laid off members of the NYC Transit Police Department was that they were all offered lower paying jobs as porters or conductors.[76]

A question regarding the ability of the Long Island Railroad Police to carry firearms resulted in a brief job action in 1971. The Railroad issued an order banning its police officers from carry firearms, so the LIRR police officers refused to report for duty. The policemen were promptly suspended by the railroad, prompting them to return to duty by the end of the day.

The railroad initially charged the policemen with having "gone AWOL" and had been prepared to seek a Federal court order against the United Transportation Union, which the railroad police were members, to ensure their return, but that proved unnecessary.

The basis for the dispute was a statement by State Attorney General Louis J. Lefkowitz the previous summer that the railroad's policemen could not legally carry firearms in the line of duty. Mr. Lefkowitz's opinion reversed those of his predecessors, who had held that the railroad's policemen did have the right to carry their .38 special revolvers.

A bill that gave the railroad policemen the right to carry firearms had passed by both houses but was still awaiting Governor Rockefeller's signature. Up until that time the Long Island railroad Police drew their authority from Railroad Law, which did not bestow New York State sworn law enforcement authority upon them. Another bill, which would give the LIRR's 105 policemen the status of "peace officers"—allowing them to make arrests and issue summonses as well as to carry firearms—was introduced by State Senator Edward J. Speno, an East Meadow, L. I., Republican.

The incident that triggered the gun ban and temporary work stoppage involved one of the LIRR. patrolmen whose revolver was confiscated by Nassau County policemen. The off duty LIRR officer also had another handgun, for which his permit had expired, and when the county policemen visited his home to check on the permit, they confiscated the weapon and his railroad-issued revolver as well. Despite Mr. Lefkowitz's opinion, the railroad policemen had continued to carry their weapons home, although they were supposed to turn them in each night, the spokesman said.

When the temporary work stoppage ended it was decided that the LIRR police would not carry guns in Nassau County. Understandably, the officers were reluctant to work without weapons. Additionally, the unions representing other LIRR workers said that the revolvers were needed to protect the crews and the commuters from people like drug addicts, derelicts and others who cause trouble on the train.

Several weeks after the dispute began, Governor Rockefeller signed a bill permitting Long Island Railroad policemen to carry pistols without a permit. It also extended the definition of peace officer to include the railroad policemen in the New York State Criminal Procedure Law.[77]

What was the job of a Long Island Railroad police officer like in the 1970s? If you asked Captain Henry Richardson, the head of the department's detective division and patrol operations, he would say it was about not being noticed.

There were times in his career when he infiltrated a gang of muggers, when he was glad to be able to move about unrecognized. But it was impossible for Captain Richardson to remain completely anonymous. He was the first railroad officer in the world to attend and graduate from the National Academy of the Federal Bureau of Investigation.

Richardson considered it a great honor to be selected for the 11-week course, and in a customary display of modesty he pointed out that the reason no railroad policeman had preceded him, was because railroads tended to be private enterprises, and the FBI did not accept trainees from the private sector.

Richardson was accepted because the FBI believed that the Long Island Railroad was different, in that it was a state entity, in affiliation with the Metropolitan Transportation Authority, making Richardson eligible.

As far as his work environment, Richardson noted that winter brought special problems for the LIRR force, which policed 345 miles of track. Winter weather sometimes caused malfunction of switching devices through vandalism. Delays from the vandalism caused crowd backups. Backups caused crowd-control problems. Captain Richardson said that because of illness and ice, there tended to be more cases of people who required assistance during the winter. He also pointed out that since it got dark early during the winter, it made things a little better for the guy that's got a little larceny in his heart.

It was a gang with larceny in its heart that first brought Officer Richardson to the attention of his superiors in 1969 after about a year and a half on the force, when he and a partner infiltrated a ring of muggers and cleared up 19 cases. He was promoted to detective and in 1971 he made sergeant. In 1974, he was promoted to lieutenant, and, a day later, to captain. Richardson was under the impression he was going to be made administrative lieutenant in the detective division, but he was shocked when he was made captain. He stressed that the choice was strictly managerial prerogative, and as shocking as it was, he certainly was not going to question an appointment to captain.

Captain Richardson believed the biggest problem that affected railroad cops was the emotional stress experienced in handling tragedies like kids getting hit, by trains - on bikes, trespassing - and all sorts of accidents.[78]

From the first time a youth threw rocks at a passing train the Long Island Railroad has dealt with acts of vandalism upon its trains, tracks and facilities. Over the years the railroad took numerous steps to reduce vandalism and trespassing and increase protection for passengers and property. One novel approach to addressing vandalism was implemented in 1971 when the railroad rented two helicopters, which patrolled the 1,000 miles of the Long Island Railroad in New York City and Nassau and Suffolk Counties, along with the 662 miles of the Hudson, Harlem and New Haven Divisions of the Penn Central.

The twin-seat helicopters, each containing a pilot and railroad policeman, regularly patrolled the track system looking for debris and for youths walking or playing on tracks just for the "fun" of it. On face value it may not have seemed like an important issue, but besides the danger involved with walking on and near the tracks, the "fun" youths frequently became involved with was sometimes throwing rocks and shooting at trains with pellet guns, and placing such objects as mattresses, 80-pound manhole covers, shopping carts, car parts, refrigerators, tubs and sinks onto the tracks.

On the LIRR vandalism knew no bounds, with incidents occurring from Manhattan and Brooklyn all the way to Montauk on the eastern end of Long Island.

During July 1972 at Hampton Bays, L. I., vandals placed a 500-pound rail on the tracks. The engine and the first four cars of a train were derailed and about 300 feet of track were torn up. Two crewmen were injured, and 125 passengers were stranded.

In another 1972 accident in Woodside, Queens, 38 persons were injured and traffic into Penn Station was delayed an hour and a half because part of wheel assembly had been damaged when it struck something on the track.

The helicopters used were rented from Decair Helicopters, Inc., of Spring Valley, N. Y. The money was obtained, by the Metropolitan Transportation Authority from the New York State Office of Crime Control Planning.

The helicopter team for the Long Island Railroad usually spotted two or three obstructions a week. If the copter was able to land nearby, the crew removed the object. If that was not possible, the police observer in the helicopter communicated by radio with any of 10

railroad police cars always in his area of operation. City and county'
policemen were also used when necessary.

When youths were seen on railroad property by the observer, who
flew at about 300 feet altitude, they were warned away by a 100-watt
public address system.

About 8,000 trespassers a year were ejected from railroad property.
The combination of the helicopter and the railroad police cars resulted
in 100 arrests a year for infractions ranging from trespassing to
disorderly conduct and criminal mischief.

The Metropolitan Transportation Authority reported that such
acts of violence as the stoning of trains and the starting of fires on
tracks had declined by more than 46 percent compared with the 12
months preceding the start of the helicopter program. The helicopters
seemed like an innovative, effective way of addressing vandalism, but
within several years the helicopter were gone. I can only assume that
the program was discontinued for financial issues because I could find
no information regarding the end of the program.[79]

The controversy regarding the ability to carry firearms was not the
only issue facing the Long Island Railroad Police during the 1970s.
1970 began with three LIRR cops standing trial for the assault of a
commuter who died several hours after the beating.

The prosecution said the policemen were called to the Savarin
Restaurant in Penn Station after the commuter, Raymond McGale of
Roosevelt, L. I., became embroiled in a fight. Mr. McGale was then
taken to the police room at the terminal. His subsequent death was
attributed to a rupture of the abdominal wall.

According to testimony at the trial Mr. McGale had been throwing
ketchup bottles and mustard jars over the bar. One prosecution
witness—a maintenance man who admitted on cross-examination that
he had been convicted "six or seven times" of various crimes—said that
before the police arrived, he had grabbed Mr. McGale from the back
and held him while another man "hit at" the commuter.

Ann McGale, the commuter's widow, also testified before the three-judge panel that one of the defendants, Patrolman John Romanewivz, told her that her husband had been given mouth-to-mouth resuscitation by the police in an effort to revive him from what appeared to be heart trouble. The other two defendants were Capt. Harry Cook, and Patrolman Wilonovsky. The three men, none of whom had been suspended from their job, were defended by lawyers hired by the Long Island Railroad Police Benevolent Association.[79]

They were eventually acquitted by the unanimous vote of a three-judge Criminal Court panel. During the four-day trial, the Manhattan District Attorney's office tried to prove that the defendants beat Mr. McGale after removing him from a brawl in the bar. No defense witnesses were called. As soon as Assistant District Attorney Allen Sullivan finished presenting his case, the defense lawyer, Marvyn Kornberg, asked for dismissal on the ground that the prosecutor had not proved his case beyond a reasonable doubt. Late in the afternoon, the judges granted the defense request.[80]

The not guilty verdict was not a complete exoneration for the police officers. Eight years later a jury in State Supreme Court in Manhattan awarded $3.3 million to McGale's widow and her four children in a civil suit against the Long Island Railroad the three officers.

Robert M. Ginsburg, the lawyer for the McGale's, said the $3.3 million was the largest settlement of a civil suit ever received in New York State. [81]

The LIRR Police K9 Unit

At Camp Milett in East Rockaway, Long Island Rail Road Lieut. James Thompson talks to children about railroad safety. The helicopter, which the children later inspected, is used by the railroad to patrol more than 1,500 miles of track. Aerial patrols are used mainly to deter trespassers.

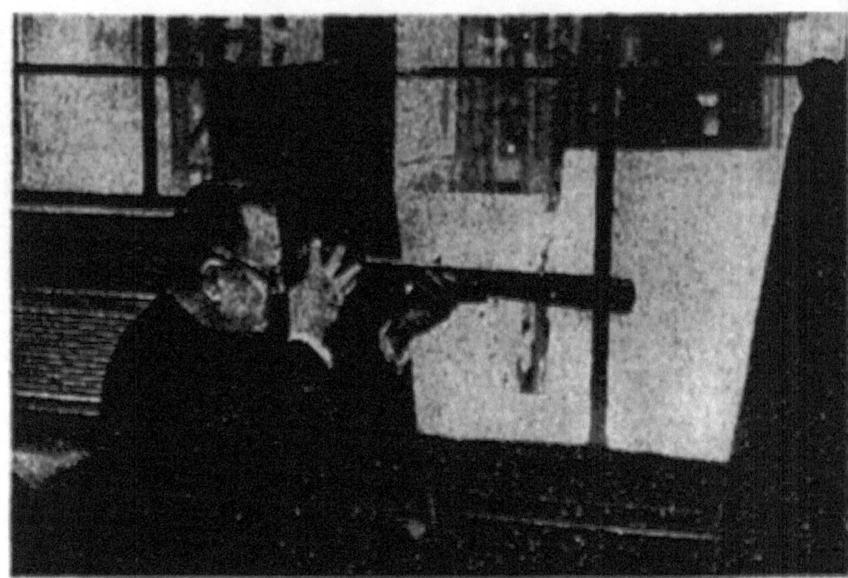

In his office on the mezzanine above the train concourse of Pennsylvania Station, Chief Frank J. Holslag of the station police can size up a situation even before it happens. He uses the spyglass to pinpoint a detail to help his officers downstairs identify a suspect.

1980 – 1998:

As the railroad entered into the1980s many railroad officials likely questioned the decision to eliminate the helicopter patrols. Vandalism continued to plague the system as the number one crime issue.

Passengers at Rockville Centre station thought there was nothing unusual about the youth on a ladder taking down public-address speakers. They believed he was an employee and suggested that he wait until the rush hour was over. In fact, he was a vandal, operating in broad daylight and undeterred by the presence of witnesses.

At the East Rockaway station, which had a raised platform at grade level, a group of youngsters ripped aside a fireproof skirt around the platform, brought in mattresses, blankets and assorted pieces of furniture and made themselves a clubhouse, replete with a campfire to keep warm.

Such vandalism at LIRR stations, which cost hundreds of thousands of dollars annually became an ever worsening problem that appeared to defy solution.

In addition to the destruction of railroad property at most of the 146 stations along 500 miles of right of way between Pennsylvania Station and Montauk, vandals frequently caused long train delays and, in a few cases, accidents.

The vandalism, which. ranged from the scrawling of initials or obscenities with cans of spray paint on walls or posters to the destruction and theft of facilities that provided comfort to passengers, was basically the work of teenagers, generally of males between 13 and 21, according to railroad officials.

The destruction, which took place mainly in the upper waiting rooms of elevated stations because the perpetrators were relatively free from observation, particularly at night, was also prevalent in street-level waiting rooms that had washrooms.

On many occasions, toilets had been clogged and plumbing ripped out, and doors inside the restrooms had been pulled loose. In the waiting rooms themselves, seats had been destroyed, wall and ceiling tiles removed, and heating equipment damaged.

At the Jamaica terminal, for example, the doors on two restroom stalls were partly ripped away, and this was in an area that was frequently patrolled by LIRR police.

At the Lindenhurst station, the handrail of the escalator was cut in two. There were beer parties in the upper-level waiting rooms, with broken bottles and cans thrown about. Doors were broken open and shopping carts were up to the platforms and thrown onto the tracks, causing delays and damage to equipment and danger to passengers.

During one winter season vandals ripped out the pipes of the heating equipment in a station, causing a potential hazard of a gas explosion. On another occasion three kids ripped out advertising billboards, took them to the upstairs waiting room and set them afire.

One of the more serious cases occurred during a snowstorm when vandals ripped apart a phone booth at the Country Life station in Garden City and threw it on the tracks. This happened during the evening rush hour, and eight eastbound trains were delayed when the New York-bound train struck the booth and was damaged."

Part of the problem was the scarcity of police to patrol the extensive area involved along the line's nine branches. The department had less than two hundred police officers, of whom only about 20 were on patrol duty in marked cars at any one time.

Beginning in January of 1980 armed LIRR police officers began patrolling trains regularly for the first time in the history of the commuter railroad. The new policy followed increased complains from citizens and crew members of serious and violent incidents. Putting officers on the trains was the second phase of an anti-crime program initiated by Chief Joseph Flynn. The first phase began two months earlier and involved patrols by plainclothes officers who worked 8-hour shifts pinpointing the trouble spots on the 322-mile system that on weekdays handled an average of 712 trains carrying 92,000 commuters and 86,000 single fare passengers.

I will pause to note a couple of facts. Joseph E. Flynn is now the Chief of the LIRR Police Department, and the listed manpower of the department has declined to 137. Chief Flynn was appointed chief in 1979 and served in that capacity for 15-years, retiring in 1994. Prior to his appointment he had retired from the New York City Police Department at the rank of Deputy Inspector.

Chief Flynn noted that since he became chief of the police force their had been a shift in priorities. Securing the yards and equipment was still critical, but he noted that security aboard trains had become an issue. He emphasized that the LIRR had a responsibility to the hardworking citizens who traveled on the trains to keep them safe. During one month of train patrol cops had made 21 arrests – one for robbery and the others for assault and disorderly conduct.[82]

In an interesting and somewhat strange announcement in 1986 Chief Flynn instituted regular police patrols on trains for what he said was the first time in the commuter line's history. This was despite the fact he had made a similar announcement six years earlier when he announced the first regular train patrols in 1980.

Chief Flynn said that the initiative was not due to a crime wave, but was intended to let the passengers know that the LIRR had a police department on the system to protect them. Some commuters, however, questioned the need for the new unit and suggested that its eight officers, could be put to better use.

"I could see it if they were assigned to help patrol Penn Station, where they are really needed," said Sheldon Schachter, a spokesman for the Long Island Railroad Commuter's Council. "They don't have that much crime on the trains to justify the patrol unit."

One thing that was new about this 1986 initiative was the increase in department manpower. In 1980 Flynn listed the department strength at 137. In this 1986 initiative, Chief Flynn said that the L.I.R.R. Police Department had increased from 135 officers in 1979, when he took command, to 215. Twelve officers just graduated from the New York City Police Academy. Five of those graduates, plus three older members of the department, formed the new patrol unit.

Flynn emphasized that he did not take away from any other units, and had built up police presence at Penn Station in recent years.

Commuters may have been critical of the new patrol strategy but the move was welcomed by the United Transportation Union, which represented 2,400 conductors and trainmen.

"I've been asking for this for years," said Edward Yule Jr., the union's general chairman. "With 185,000 people a day riding the trains you're going to have your share of trouble, so a uniformed cop is a big help."

When the new unit went on duty, it began patrolling about 100 trains a week before increasing to more than 200 a week. Chief Flynn said, "We want our presence to assure the commuter of a feeling of safety, and to deter any would-be wrongdoers from engaging in any type of criminal act or annoyance."

The first statistics for the new patrol initiative reflected that between Jan. 9 and Jan. 31, the unit responded to 47 calls for assistance, of which 26 took place on trains, 18 at stations and three along the tracks.

A total of 458 trains were patrolled, and 15 criminal summonses were issued. There were two arrests, one for pulling an emergency cord and another for disorderly conduct. The unit also handled 14 fare disputes without an arrest being made. It also helped to return three young children to their parents, aided a homeless man who was stabbed by another homeless man in Pennsylvania Station, and called relatives of two intoxicated passengers, who came and took them home.

This train patrol initiative was a shift from the normal uniformed patrol strategy of the LIRR Police Department. Officers were regularly stationed at Penn Station, Jamaica, and Flatbush Avenue, while the outlying stations and track areas were patrolled by radio cars, and anti-crime units worked undercover conducting surveillance.[83]

In 1966 the LIRR was taken over by the State of New York and made a ward of New York's Metropolitan Transportation Authority (MTA). An important statement was made at the time of the State takeover by the leadership of the railroad—"We just have a new owner and a new board of directors. We're under the Railway Labor Act, just as we've always been. The people do not become state employees, they remain railroad employees."

The importance of that statement could not be understated. Another ward of the MTA was the New York City Transit Authority. In the same year the state purchased the LIRR, all subway service was halted for 12 days by a strike. In response, the state legislature passed the Public Employees Fair Employment Act, commonly referred to as the Taylor Law, which outlaws strikes by public-employee unions and requires binding arbitration to settle wage, benefits, and work rules disputes.

For 13 years, the state-owned LIRR and its unions bargained under provisions of the Federal Railway Labor Act (RLA). But in 1979, with a work stoppage on LIRR looming, the state did an about-face and challenged RLA coverage, seeking to invoke the more restrictive Taylor Law. In a case that reached the U.S. Supreme Court, it was held that, "To allow individual states, by acquiring railroads, to circumvent the federal system of collective bargaining . . . would destroy the longstanding and comprehensive scheme of federal regulation of railroads and their labor relations thought essential by Congress."

So it was that LIRR labor-management relations remained governed by the RLA and its long and drawn-out procedures that could avert work stoppages—but that did, unlike the Taylor Law, eventually permit a lawful strike. The difference between the two laws was crucial, because when Local 100 of the Transport Workers Union struck New York's subway system for two days in 2005, in violation of the Taylor Law, a federal judge sentenced the local's president to 10 days in jail and fined the union $2.5 million. Of course, LIRR management would prefer that LIRR be governed by the Taylor Law, which could shrink a truculent union's treasury small enough to fit in a conductor's lunch pail.

Under the RLA, when parties failed to reach a voluntary settlement—and either side declined binding arbitration—a fact-finding Presidential Emergency Board (PEB) could be appointed to make non-binding settlement recommendations. The RLA was amended by Congress in 1981 to provide that if the sides in a commuter rail dispute could not settle voluntarily based on the first PEB's recommendations, a second PEB would be created at the request of either party. PEBs were designed to create public pressure on the parties to settle voluntarily.

The first PEB—as it does with freight railroads and Amtrak—makes non-binding recommendations. The second PEB, for commuter railroads only, asks each side to submit its last best offer, making a non-binding choice as to which offer it considers the most reasonable.

Since the 1981 RLA amendment providing for a second PEB in commuter rail disputes, there had been only two commuter railroad work stoppages following failed wage, benefits, and work rules negotiations—both on LIRR.

In 1987, there was an 11-day LIRR work stoppage, with Congress creating, during the strike, the equivalent of a third PEB—called an advisory board—that led to a settlement.[84]

Workers walked off their jobs early on January 18, 1987, shutting down the nation's busiest commuter line. The strike came after several days of around-the-clock negotiations that resulted in Joseph A. Cassidy Jr., General Chairman of the Brotherhood of Locomotive Engineers, one of 11 unions attempting to negotiate a new contract, saying they had reached an "irreconcilable impasse" with the railroad.

Officials of the railroad's police union announced that their members would also strike, and the railroad halted operations. Meanwhile officials said local police departments would guard trains stored in the line's yards.

Under the Federal Railway Labor Act, two Presidential panels had attempted to resolve the dispute and two 120-day cooling-off periods had elapsed. A few months into the strike, five of the line's unions - representing conductors, clerks, ticket sellers, yard masters and supervisors - had accepted a new contract that provided for a wage increase of about 20 percent over 4 1/2 years, retroactive to 1985. But unions representing 60 percent of the line's 6,600 organized workers - including engineers, machinists, carmen, boilermakers, laborers, electricians, sheet-metal workers, track workers, signalmen, police officers and supervisors - rejected that offer.

Stuart Sanseviro, president of the Police Benevolent Association, said the railroad had demanded that his union agree to work during a strike. "My self-respect was at stake," he said.[85]

President Reagan reluctantly became involved in the strike when he signed a Congressional Decree ordering the striking employees back to their jobs during the 60-day cooling off period. In signing the back-to-work law, President Reagan said in a statement, "The urgency with which this legislation was passed reflects the enormous hardship visited upon the citizens of the communities served by the Long Island Railroad."

The unions honored the order, and some workers began returning to work that same night. The President's back to work order came just Mr. Sanseviro had reached an agreement for the police union's arbitration.[86]

As more of the Metropolitan Area population moved out to the suburbs more commuters used the Long Island Railroad. More commuters meant more cars in the LIRR's parking lots, and more of a menu for car thieves to select from. The situation came to a head in

1989 with the tragic death of 15-year-old Brian Benson. The youth, from North Great River, was riding his bike down Connetquot Avenue, when a Mazda, which had been stolen from a nearby LIRR station by two Central Islip teens ran off the road during a pursuit by police and hit the boy, killing him. The tragedy prompted the Suffolk County Police and LIRR Police to initiate "Operation Zebra."

In two weeks of surveillance Operation Zebra resulted in the arrest of 15 suspects and the recovery of ten stolen vehicles from the Central Islip, Brentwood and Deer Park railroad stations. Since the electrification of the Ronkonkoma line ridership had increased along with the number of complaints of stolen vehicles and vandalism of parked cars. The joint operation between the Suffolk and LIRR Police Departments came about as a result of community leaders banding together after the Brian Benson tragedy to seek help from police to ebb the flow of stolen vehicles from the LIRR parking lots. The LIRR reported a 30% increase in stolen vehicles from their parking lots over a one-year period. These thefts, like car thefts everywhere, fell into three categories. Some cars were stolen by joy riders and others to strip for parts. Still others boosted the vehicles to sell the whole car on the market.

The extent of the problem was first discovered several months earlier when LIRR Police apprehended five juveniles ranging in age from 13-17 for stealing seven cars from area railroad parking lots. The suspects used the cars for their own amusement in a demolition derby which they held near the Central Islip State Hospital grounds. According to LIRR Police Captain Frank Obremski, ridership specifically on the Ronkonkoma line doubled over a two year period requiring more parking lots and larger lots. He said that the larger the parking lot the easier it is for the car thieves.[87]

Like all the preceding decades the 1990s brought problems at grade crossings. Gone were the days of crossing watchmen fixed at a crossing.

Now, the police dispatched officers in patrol cars to crossings needing enforcement.

Shortly after 4 PM on a Thursday, Officer Fred Benz of the Long Island Railroad Police Department sat in his patrol car at a grade crossing in New Hyde Park. He heard the familiar ringing of bells, a signal that the railroad gates were being activated because a train was approaching. Four seconds later, the gates began to descend. At the same time Officer Benz saw a red Ford Mustang accelerate around the gates and cross the track, almost hitting the gates. He followed the driver for three blocks, until the car stopped at a light at Jericho Turnpike, where Officer Benz signaled the driver to pull over. After being told of the offense, the 30-year-old driver, from Queens, matter-of-factly accepted a summons, which called for a minimum fine of $150. The driver was also told that he would have to appear in Central Traffic Court in Hempstead.[88]

During the 1987 strike negotiations, wages and benefits were the main items on the police union's agenda, but police union president Sanveriro trumpeted a common theme. He called the trains "unsafe" and said the railroad needed to triple the size of its 216-person police force. Railroad officials responded by pointing out that the rate of crime against passengers had dropped over the last few years. Several years later the need to increase the size of the Long Island Railroad Police Department would take center stage – in a dramatic and tragic fashion.

On a spring day in 1993 a man walked into a hunting and fishing store in Southern California to buy a 15-shot semiautomatic pistol. He selected a bulky Ruger P-89, a weapon designed for the military, gave his real name, supplied a California driver's license with a Long Beach address, affirmed that he was not a convicted felon or a mental patient and was told he could pick up the weapon after a waiting period of sixteen days. Fifteen days were imposed by the state of California, and one was added for good measure by the gun store.

The owner of the store noticed nothing odd about his customer who put down a deposit of $82 for the pistol, which was on sale for $299. When the sixteen days had passed the man paid the balance due and departed with the gun. He was not heard from again until the early evening of December 7, 1993, on board a Long Island Railroad train that had just pulled out of the New Hyde Park station in Nassau County. The next stop was Merrilon Avenue in Garden City.[89]

The 34-year-old-woman was trying to relax in her seat as best as she could. She was seven-and-a-half months pregnant and every day the ride home from Manhattan to Long Island became progressively more fatiguing. When the train pulled out of New Hyde Park she closed her eyes in a vain attempt to sleep. Her eyes popped opened at the sound of the door at the end of the car opening. Someone had entered the car.

The woman watched in horror as Colin Ferguson calmly began walking down the length of the car, swinging his gun from right to left as he fired upon the helpless passengers. The woman got into a fetal position on the floor to protect her baby. Then she felt the bullet strike her.[90]

Andrew Roderick stood on the platform at Merillon Avenue. He was standing where the third car stopped, his usual location for meeting his wife when she got off the 5:33 out of Penn Station. The off duty Long Island Railroad Police Officer had no idea he was about to become involved in one the most infamous crimes committed on the railroad.

When the train pulled into the station the 27-year-old Roderick knew something was wrong. The doors did not open and he could hear screams from inside the train. Some people emerged on the platform from an open door and screamed that someone was shooting on the train. Upon hearing that there was a gunman on the train, Officer Roderick felt torn between concern for his wife's safety and his law-enforcement duty, but he realized he had to respond to the man with a gun.[91]

Roderick banged on the train door, shouting that he was a police officer and for someone to open the door. He heard no shots being fired so he still wasn't sure what had happened. But as soon as the doors opened, the bloodbath inside told the story clearly. He saw people crouched in their seats, and he saw the bodies. Some passengers were slumped over while others cried and screamed.

Roderick had missed the killing spree and he also missed the heroic actions of three passengers who had charged Ferguson when he stopped shooting to reload. When Roderick entered the car the three heroes had Ferguson pinned to the floor. Roderick ran out of the train and retrieved a pair of handcuffs from an arriving police car. Roderick ran back to the car, handcuffed Ferguson and removed him from the train. As he placed the handcuffs on, Ferguson calmly stated, "Yeah, I did it. I'm not going anywhere."

When the carnage was over Ferguson had shot 25-people in the car. Six were dead and nineteen were wounded. The pregnant woman recovered, and her baby was born several weeks later. Colin Ferguson was sentenced to 315-years in prison.[92]

After the shooting everyone seemed to be in agreement that more cops were needed on LIRR trains. The problem was that it would be a near impossible job to place a cop on every train. When I was a member of the New York City Transit Police, the department attempted to put a cop on every subway train, and it was a challenge even for a department with over three thousand cops. The Long Island railroad had just over 200 cops which translated into about twenty cops on duty on a shift throughout the entire massive area where the railroad serviced, operating 740 trains a day for 256,000 riders.

Since the LIRR was not going to hire thousands of officers, Governor George Pataki endorsed another plan. On August 3, 1995, with survivors of the Long Island Railroad massacre looking over his shoulder, the Governor signed a law allowing police officers to travel on the railroad without charge. The decision was hailed by all, especially since there seemed to be no real cost associated with it, and with off duty police riding the trains, no one would ever know whether they were sitting next to a policeman or not.

The law covered officers employed by New York City, Nassau and Suffolk Counties, the State Police, the Port Authority, the Metro-North Commuter Railroad and municipalities on Long Island.

Since 7,600 members of the New York City police force lived on Long Island, it was estimated that 5,000 could possibly make use of the new free transportation. There were an additional 3,000 officers living in Queens who could also take advantage of the free fare.

It was a good deal for the public because these officers took an oath to protect life and property and were well-trained to do just that.

This program seemed like a win-win for all, but there were a couple of issues. First, there were no statistics to say how many additional off duty officers would ride the railroad because of the free fare. Some in the LIRR feared that there were already thousands of off duty cops riding the rails, and that all this program would result in were less fares collected from a segment of the ridership previously paying. The second issue had to do with the conductors. I was a recipient of a police pass when the program began in 1995, and because the police passes were white in color, it was very easy for the conductor to identify an off duty officer. I have much respect and affection of LIRR conductors. In fact, my son is an LIRR conductor. However, once the free fare program began, I heard several stories of conductors acting in a manner I did not understand. One of the regulations of the program was that an off duty officer would not take a seat if a paying customer was standing. I was told of experiences from several different friends who were ordered by conductors to stand, even though there was no one standing at the time. I had a personal experience with the other major complaint I heard. I don't think any cop needed a free fare to take action when action needed to be taken, but some of these conductors seemed to relish the idea that they had their own private bouncers on board to do their bidding. For example, one evening I was taking the railroad home when an announcement came over the PA system – "Police officer to the second car."

I was several cars back so as I begin moving forward, I was wondering what the condition is. Was there someone with a gun? Was there an assault or robbery taking place?

When I entered the second car everything appeared quiet and normal. The conductor marched over to me, pointed to a man standing in the vestibule and announced, "that guy was smoking. Write him a summons."

The man in the vestibule looked at me and shrugged. "Yeah, I was smoking, and he told me to put it out, so I did."

I turned to the conductor. "He's not smoking now."

The conductor grew agitated. "He was smoking. and he admitted it. Write him a summons."

My agitation was growing. "I don't know if you realize it, but we don't carry summonses off duty. Additionally, smoking on the train is a violation. I can only write a summons for a violation that I witnessed." I pointed at the conductor as the train pulled into Floral Park. "Only you can sign the summons since you witnessed the violation. If you would like, you can hold the train here until the Floral Park Police Department responds and they can issue a summons that you sign."

"Ah, forget it," he snarled.[94]

Five months after the shooting, Long Island Railroad officials clashed with critics over the extent of crime on the railroad. While railroad officials acknowledged at a public meeting that there were problems in the parking lots and the areas surrounding the stations, they said that their count of 289 felonies committed throughout the rail system in 1993 was the lowest number in more than a decade and that car thefts had dropped substantially in the last year.

Charles Hoppe, the railroad's president, said, "On our trains, there was one chance in 850,000 that a customer would be involved in a crime," and he noted that surveys had shown that riders generally viewed the Ferguson shooting as a tragic aberration.

But representatives of the Long Island Railroad Police Benevolent Association countered that the railroad's information was misleading. Raymond W. Gimmler Jr., a union vice president, said police departments in Riverhead, Long Beach and Malverne had reported more than twice the number of crimes at their stations than the railroad police had recorded.

The dispute arose at a meeting convened by State Senator Norman J. Levy, chairman of the Senate Transportation Committee, to discuss possible changes in how the railroad fought crime. While the railroad's problems with crimes had been highlighted by the Ferguson shooting, Mr. Levy said that even months before that, commuters were expressing concerns to him about car thefts and safety problems on platforms and in waiting rooms at the railroad's 103 stations and parking lots.

During the 1990s, the railroad police had taken on more of the responsibility of protecting cars in station lots, a job traditionally left to local police forces. But the railroad still relied heavily on local police departments to patrol these areas.

LIRR Police Chief Flynn said that the railroad had to assume a moral responsibility to protect its customers in these areas, and he announced that the 223-person force would receive 16 more officers to strengthen its station patrols. Still, with a jurisdiction stretching from New York City to Montauk, some law-enforcement officials noted that this was still far too few officers to monitor all of its stations adequately without substantial support from local police forces.

Mr. Gimmler of the railroad police union called the move inadequate, arguing that the local police forces were overburdened and could not pay enough attention to the stations. He called for the railroad to hire 200 more officers during the next two years.

Although much of the meeting was devoted to the issues of station safety, it could not avoid the question of whether the railroad could have done anything to have stopped Colin Ferguson. Chief Flynn said that it would not work to increase patrols to try to stop such a random crime.[95]

Transportation systems will always be attractive terrorist targets, but the Long Island railroad Police discovered that their involvement went beyond the tracks and stations in the LIRR system.

On a morning in 1997 two men with Jordanian passports were arrested in a Brooklyn apartment, where police officers found components of one or more pipe bombs—evidence of what the authorities said was a terrorist plot to detonate bombs in the busy Atlantic Avenue subway station and on a commuter bus.

The two suspects were shot after a team of New York City police officers, acting on a tip from a man who lived with the two, burst into the Park Slope apartment an hour before dawn. The police said they opened fire when one of the men appeared to be trying to set off one of the explosive devices. Federal law enforcement officials said the police had recovered a nine-inch pipe packed with gunpowder and nails, and a device in which four pipes had been wrapped together and equipped with toggle-switch detonators. Three high-ranking investigators said that the lack of a timer or a remote-control detonator on the device strongly suggested that it was intended for a suicide attack.

Police Commissioner Howard Safir said the material was powerful enough to kill anyone within 25 feet of detonation in an enclosed space.

The events began unfolding with the frantic waving of a stranger along a darkened Brooklyn street. Mohammed Chindluri flagged down a Long Island Railroad police car at 10:45 P.M. and tried to explain, in Arabic, that disaster was imminent. He repeatedly screamed "Bomba," as he cupped his hands and flung them apart to mimic an explosion. The LIRR officer in the police car brought the man to the 88th Precinct station house in Fort Greene where an interpreter was summoned to translate his story. The man said that several men living in an apartment at 248 Fourth Avenue were planning to blow up subways and buses in New York City. The New York City police soon set into motion an often-rehearsed plan of attack. By early morning, a team of Emergency Service Unit officers began to close in on the four-story building.

That stretch of Fourth Avenue, between Carroll and President Streets, was a mishmash of the residential and commercial; there were automotive-supply stores, a construction company, an after-hours club, a few bodegas and several apartments atop first-floor storefronts. In the midst of it all was a two-story study in neglect, with paint peeling and windows ajar: 248 Fourth Avenue. It housed the Family Car Service in front and had apartments in the back and above. The men who lived in the apartment behind the storefront, including the suspects, were described as poor, friendly when spoken to, unassuming.

The predawn raid was like a scene out of a movie. The police officers entered an apartment cast in darkness, save for the light from their flashlights. There they found one man in the front room, and two in the back bedroom. In the maelstrom of shouts and screams, the police said one man reached for an officer's gun while the other moved toward a black bag, which later was found to contain an electronic device. The police opened fire, wounding two of the suspects.

At daybreak, the investigation was in full gear, headed by the Joint Terrorist Task Force, with New York City detectives and agents from the F.B.I. and the Bureau of Alcohol, Tobacco and Firearms.[96]

Eventually, investigators linked the suspects in the raid to the radical Palestinian group Hamas. They were believed to have made telephone calls to the organization from a grocery store and a launderette in the neighborhood.

One of the suspects told bomb squad experts how to dismantle the recovered bombs. It was he who told police they planned to detonate the bombs in the subway.[97]

As the Long Island Railroad moved through the 1990s, its police department had developed into a modern, professional agency of well-trained police officers.

The LIRR was reaching its height as a high-volume commuter railway serving the greater New York Metropolitan Area. It was the nation's largest commuter rail system, serving an area of nearly 4,000 square miles containing a population of 12 million. Each week, the LIRR made 318,000 trips on over 700 route miles of track, almost 400 of which were electrified. About 75,000,000 passengers used the system each year during the decade of the 1990s. An average of 700,000 passengers used the 134 train stations each day. In suburban Long Island, 403 parking lots adjacent to passenger stations allowed patrons in Nassau and Suffolk counties to drive to the LIRR in order to board a train to New York City. The Long Island Railroad had come a long way since the 19th century, and so had the Long Island Railroad Police Department. Even the reorganized police force of 1904 was no comparison to the modern LIRR police department of the 1990s.

After the reorganization of the department in 1904, LIRR Police Officers were designated police officers, but their authority was very limited in its scope. Prior to changes in the Criminal Procedure Law in 1970, which specifically listed individual agencies whose employees are police officers, LIRR officers were empowered under Section 88 of the New York State Railroad Law, which authorizes railroads to employ police officers and to apply for state-sanctioned police authorization on behalf of those employees.

Prior to 1970, the antiquated Railroad Law, dating back to the late 1800s, prevented the very qualified officers of the LIRR Police Department from exercising their police authority except when they were acting on or in connection with property that was connected with or under the control of the railroad company for which they worked. This rigid territorial limitation on their police power, which was rooted in historical and outdated legislation, was highly unsuitable for law enforcement in the modern world. The current language of the Railroad Law existed in its present form as of 1968, but the vast majority of the language existed as far back as 1924, and the original geographic limitations on railroad policemen's powers most likely date all the way back to 1890. Although there very well could have been a rational purpose behind the Legislature's decision to treat railroad police officers differently from other police officers back in 1890, 1910, and perhaps even 1924, it was evident that this historical anachronism simply remained in place over the following decades while the Legislature turned its focus to new areas of concern. [98]

Even with full New York State police powers, other agencies played a big role in policing the railroad. The New York City Police Department, as well as either the Nassau and Suffolk County police departments had primary (or original) and concurrent jurisdiction with the Long Island Railroad Police Department along various parts of the system. A number of smaller municipal police agencies also served portions of the system and shared jurisdiction on railroad property within their communities. This concurrent jurisdiction was essential because the local police agencies were often in a much better position to respond quickly to an LIRR incident within their town or city. Additionally, although the Long Island Railroad Police Department officers were well trained, and several specialized units existed, the department did not possess all the resources necessary to deal with every criminal and emergency situation like a larger agency like the NYPD did.

During the 1990s the LIRR Police Department focused its specialized policing in areas of the greatest concern to their customers. Auto theft and vehicle burglaries at parking facilities was a concern at transit facilities throughout the United States. Parking lot crime, in fact, could influence patron acceptance of a transit system. As a result, patron perceptions of parking lot security were an important indicator of overall system performance. One of the ways the LIRR discovered what its customers were concerned about was through the administration of annual Customer Satisfaction Surveys. These surveys covered a wide range of topics from cleanliness of facilities and availability of timetables to lighting at the stations and personal security.

As early as 1991 customers began expressing concern about parking lot security and auto-related thefts. As a result of this input, the LIRR Police began to deploy officers to selected parking lots, making a substantial number of arrests (65 in 1991 and 125 in 1992). The overwhelming majority of these arrests were for auto related crimes, specifically either theft of the auto itself (Grand Larceny-Auto) or thefts from parked vehicles. Although police activity to combat auto-related crimes was increasing, the volume of this form of crime was also increasing. By 1993, it was determined that a separate, dedicated Auto Crime Unit should be established to address parking lot crime.

The December 7, 1993 shooting on a Long Island Rail Road train that resulted in six deaths and a number of injuries focused public concern on commuter safety and security at the LIRR. During legislative hearings held in the shooting's aftermath, public concern shifted from on-board crime to security at parking lots. According to LIRR Police Chief John J. O'Connor, parking lot safety and security was an important element in improving passenger perceptions of safety.

A quick side note – John J. O'Connor replaced Chief Flynn in 1994.

Surveys showed that the stereotypical "Dashing Dan," was no longer the primary customer. Ridership was 40 percent female. As a result, parking lot safety became a more important issue since women frequently reported feeling less safe than did male commuters in these areas.

The LIRR Police established the Auto Crime Unit (ACU) in January 1994. With an initial complement of one sergeant and four police officers, a continuing focus on parking lot security was initiated. Charles Hoppe, then President of the LIRR, endorsed the unit, stating, "Serving our customers means providing a strong deterrent to auto crime in the parking lots at our stations, as well as other critical aspects of improving our service." From its inception, the ACU recognized that it must have a dual mission if it was going to be effective in reducing parking lot crime. Law enforcement was the obvious approach, but ACU members believed this would prove most effective if paired with commuter education.

The primary law enforcement activity adopted by the ACU was an arrest-oriented tactic—the plainclothes surveillance of parking lots by teams of officers. The educational aspect included providing crime awareness and prevention presentations to community and commuter groups. Members of the unit also distributed pamphlets to passengers at a number of rail stations, and provided crime prevention tips to reduce auto crime in parking lot.

By 1996, the ACU had expanded to eight police officers, two detectives and a detective sergeant. It was headed by a detective lieutenant. Prior to the establishment of the ACU, LIRR officers had no specialized training or equipment to support their effectiveness. Once the unit was established, each officer and supervisor attended the New York City Police Department Auto Crime School. Each officer was also trained in utilizing LOJACK (a commercial stolen vehicle recovery system), mobile digital terminal (MDT) operations, plainclothes officer safety, and emergency vehicle operation. Auto Crime Unit officers were equipped with multi-channel radios to speed interagency communications. Two laptop computers were assigned to the unit to serve as MDTs which provided direct access to the New York State Police Information Network (NYSPIN). This allowed officers to conduct rapid vehicle checks and wanted person inquiries directly, avoiding the need to route checks through headquarters personnel, potentially delaying the inquiry process.

In order to conduct surveillance undetected by auto thieves, members of the unit needed to have cars that were not obviously police vehicles. Insurance companies were called upon to support ACU efforts in this regard. As part of this approach, insurance carriers agreed to provide a variety of vehicles to the unit for use in counter theft operations. These vehicles had been reported stolen, were later recovered, and the owners had already been compensated for their loss. Insurance companies enlisted by the ACU included Allstate, GEICO, Travelers, Liberty Mutual, Utica Mutual, Commercial Union, Metropolitan, Nationwide, and U.S. Capital. Each had a "vehicle lender program" which enabled the company to provide vehicles to the ACU for a one-year period. The vehicles could be replaced or renewals extended if both the ACU and insurance company agreed. As of the summer of 1996, thirteen vehicles had been obtained by the Auto Crime Unit. Two of these were permanently donated to the LIRR Police.

One of the most vexing problems faced by ACU officers at the inception of their effort was understanding the extent and type of crimes they were facing. Criminal complaints and arrests were generally not made directly to the LIRR Police, but rather to the police agency (county or municipal police) where the crime occurred. While these other police agencies recorded and tabulated crime statistics for their own departments, they generally did not segregate crime committed on LIRR property or advise LIRR Police of these incidents. Members of the ACU recognized the need to identify and then develop a rapport with their colleagues at these external police agencies in order to acquire the data needed to effectively contain parking lot crime affecting the system.

With the cooperation of these often overlapping agencies, LIRR officers could not only get the data they needed, but they could get it on a weekly basis. The external agencies were quite willing to assist LIRR Police data collection efforts, since reducing crime at parking lots translated into reduced crime in their policing area and fewer complaints from members of the communities they served. In order to maintain and strengthen rapport with these other police agencies, joint auto theft operations were periodically conducted by members of the LIRR Auto Crime Unit and their counterparts at these agencies.

Armed with the necessary crime statistics, the Auto Crime Unit was able to establish priorities and monitor the impact of its deployment strategies. Chief O'Connor placed the results of ACU efforts into the following context: "Anytime in police work that you make a 10 percent impact, you've accomplished something."

For the calendar year 1993 (the year prior to the formation of the Auto Crime Unit), the LIRR experienced 676 vehicle thefts and police made 94 arrests. In 1994, vehicle thefts dropped 30 percent to 474, while arrests rose 71 percent to 161. This trend continued for 1995 when vehicle thefts dropped another 29 percent to 335 and arrests rose an additional 8 percent to 174.

Since the Auto Crime Unit's inception, vehicle thefts dropped 50 percent, while arrests rose 85 percent. Just as prior to the inception of the specialized unit, arrests continued to be overwhelmingly auto-crime related. Unit members, though, have found that a number of suspects taken into custody for these crimes were found to be wanted for previous crimes or to have information about other serious crimes in the immediate area. The ability to focus on the target crime, to become familiar with a number of the offenders' patterns, and to work more closely with local police resulted in some suspects being charged with other, non-railroad related crimes or in those with knowledge of other crimes providing information to local police in return for consideration on their current charges. Thus, although the ACU did not keep these as separate statistics, targeted police efforts resulted in related arrests and opened new lines of communication with police departments whose jurisdictions overlapped that of the LIRR officers.

Clearly the Auto Crime Unit was doing something right and meeting Chief O'Connor's definition of accomplishment.

Until problem-oriented policing and community policing began to be embraced by police agencies, the typical response to rising auto theft was generally an increased deployment of officers to parking lots with the mandate to make more arrests. There was no doubt that this was a useful strategy, and one that the LIRR Police Department certainly employed. Yet this approach did not involve the potential victims in the process. Individuals were unlikely to think of target hardening on their own. All that most commuters wanted to do at a train station was find parking spaces for their cars and catch their trains on time. Their focus was on the train, not the car. To assist commuters in target hardening, the ACU officers analyzed criminal complaints. Their research indicated that the most frequently stolen items from cars were AM/FM cassette players, cellular phones, airbags, valuables such as cameras left in plain sight, and license plates.

A thief could not covet what he did not see. ACU officers prepared a brief guide of auto theft prevention tips, which they handed out at train stations in the morning hours to commuters as they boarded their trains. This also provided ACU officers with the opportunity to interact briefly with commuters, providing visible indication that the railroad was responding to commuter concerns about parking lot safety in general and auto-related thefts in particular. Officers also attended community meetings, distributing the prevention tips and discussing other issues of concern to commuters. Moreover, they advised members of the public to lock their cars (13 percent of stolen vehicles had the keys in the car) and to hide valuables from sight (but not under the seat which was one of the first places a thief would check). In addition, they recommended that members of the public not leave a license, registration, or title inside the vehicle since this facilitated the sale of a stolen car. Finally, officers suggested that a car should be parked with its wheels turned sharply to the right or left and the emergency brake applied to make it difficult to tow the car away.

ACU officers walked up and down the aisles of parking lots looking into cars to see if valuables were visible or if the car door was open. When they encountered such cars (some of which had change or dollar bills in plain sight), they left their business cards on the car advising the owner on the back of the card that this time it was a police officer who had observed the crime-prone condition, but it could just as easily have been a thief.

The ACU also incorporated a "Combat Auto Theft" (CAT) program into its overall prevention strategy. The CAT program was initially started by the New York City Police Department in a pilot program instituted in the borough of Queens during the 1980s. Designed to combat a dramatic rise in auto larcenies, the NYPD program was initially geared to thefts that occurred during overnight hours, but it was expanded to include cars parked in the street during daylight hours.

The LIRR Police CAT program involved a car owner signing a statement that the car was parked at a commuter lot Monday through Friday between the hours of 9:00 a.m. and 5:00 p.m. and gave law enforcement officers consent to stop the vehicle if it was observed being operated during those hours. By signing up for CAT, the vehicle owner provided police with probable cause to stop the vehicle even though no infraction had been observed. Vehicles in the CAT program displayed a special sticker so police knew the car was enrolled in the program.

VIN etching was another voluntary program in which the public could participate to reduce the likelihood of their vehicles being stolen. In this program, a car's 17-character vehicle identification number (VIN) was etched (using acids and stencils) into the major glass components of the vehicle. While the street value of an average stolen vehicle was about $300 or $400, a vehicle that had been VIN etched dropped in value to approximately $100. The Auto Crime Unit also developed a program known as "Adopt a Station" in which ACU officers were individually assigned to stations experiencing the highest levels of crime. This deployment was based on detailed analysis of crime activity at all commuter parking lots. As part of this precision targeting, each officer monitored crime patterns and played a key role in devising problem-solving strategies aimed at reducing crime.

Even with enhanced staffing, the ACU had only ten officers and detectives assigned to prevent or reduce crime in the one hundred plus parking lots spread throughout two of the nation's most populous counties. The railroad right-of-way traversed 701 miles over 11 branches; travelling through three counties of New York City (Manhattan, Brooklyn, and Queens) and Nassau and Suffolk counties. Some of the parking lots were small to moderate in size, accommodating one or two hundred vehicles. Others, such as Ronkonkoma Station, had parking for several thousand cars. For example, there were four separate entrances to the Ronkonkoma complex of lots, and some of them were isolated from the station itself. In total, nearly 50,000 cars were parked in Long Island Railroad lots in Nassau and Suffolk counties on a typical, non-holiday weekday.

To cope with this volume, the ACU occasionally deployed an unmarked surveillance van capable of covertly observing and recording criminal activity. At some stations, the unit also had mounted covert cameras at the top of utility poles, which were monitored from remote locations. Despite these high-tech tools, most monitoring was carried out by an officer equipped with nothing more technically advanced than binoculars and a radio. Officers assigned as observers scanned the parking lots for indicators of potential crime, including behavior that was out of the ordinary. The parking lots filled up quite rapidly, so when an officer saw a car passing up an empty parking spot the officer took notice. Officers also took note when a car was casually driving up and down lanes as a train was pulling into the station. This behavior was atypical, since most commuters tried as quickly as possible to find a spot and catch their train. For the same reasons, a car driven slowly and containing multiple occupants also attracted heightened scrutiny. In addition, officers looked for the typical signs of parking lot crime. These included vent windows that had been blown out or side windows opened on a cold day, as well as a door lock popped or a key in the ignition. Officers also noted carefully the position of any keys they observed in ignitions, since this may have indicated that the key was non-functioning and that the vehicle had been hot-wired. Adding to the challenges facing the unit was the lack of a consistent profile of offenders, who ranged in age from their early teens to their sixties. Arrested subjects could dress casually or in suits. Some even carried briefcases. One twelve-year-old was observed systematically walking through each row of parked cars in a lot, a radio in one hand and a screw driver in the other. When questioned by the police, he admitted that his stepfather had sent him into the lot to determine if LIRR Police were present. There are also a variety of motives for committing crime in the lots. Some teenagers wanted to steal a car for a joyride or to impress their friends. Others wanted to steal valuables from the vehicles. Some stole cars to sell for a few hundred dollars; others stole the cars for their parts. Some had no particular car type in mind, but saw what opportunity presented itself. Others knew in advance what model and year of car they wanted.

With most commuters away for eight, ten, or more hours a day and thousands of cars to choose from, commuter parking lots were certainly tempting targets. The police officers chosen for the Auto Crime Unit were hand-picked for the assignment and viewed their selection as an indicator of skill and competence. The unit was extremely active; high-quality arrests were made, conviction rates were high, and officers believed they were having an impact on crime. Chief O'Connor believed that at least part of the high morale could be attributed to the policy of allowing officers to use their surveillance cars to commute to and from work, providing them with a chance to use a late model, often highly costly and popular car they would otherwise rarely get to drive. While officers could use the cars in this manner, they were not permitted to use them during their off-duty hours. He noted that this policy had not resulted in an increase in auto accidents, and that, in fact, the first accident involving a loaned vehicle did not occur until eighteen months into the program. The few accidents that had occurred were all enforcement related, with none having taken place while officers were on their own time. The officers worked as members of an elite team and started each day with a strategy briefing, determining which lots they would cover during their shift. They learned not to broadcast that information over their radios once deployed, since some criminals monitored the police bands and could find out which lots would not be frequented by the police that day.

The Auto Crime Unit achieved an impressive reduction in the number of auto and auto-related thefts in the parking lots on which it concentrated. [99]

The Auto Crime Unit was reflective of the highly trained police department fielded by the Long Island railroad during the final years of the 20th century. But it wasn't only the members of ACU who were highly trained.

In 1997 The Long Island Railroad Police Department had a strength of 220 sworn police officers with an annual police budget of $19 million. Uniformed patrols were employed to meet trains and to monitor stations and railway facilities. Vehicle patrols were used to respond to incidents. A number of plainclothes operations addressed vandalism, graffiti, pickpocketing, and illegal dumping on LIRR right-of-way. The LIRR Police Department also maintained a detective bureau which conducted criminal investigations in support of the overall system security and crime control mission.

For all LIRR police officers training began with recruit police academy training. The LIRR did not maintain a police academy. Officers received recruit training either with the New York City,

Nassau, or Suffolk County Police Departments, and with some additional LIRR topics given by LIRR police instructors after graduation, they received far in excess of the New York State Municipal Police Training Council's minimum of 520 hours of basic training.

In 1993 talks regarding merging the New York City Transit and Housing police departments into the NYPD began to heat up. For many years up to that point the Transit Police had conducted recruit academy training in the same manner as the LIRR police. They sent their recruits to the New York City Police Academy. In a move to try to distant itself from a possible merger, the Transit Police pulled out of the NYPD Police Academy and opened its own police academy, taking the LIRR and Metro North police departments along for the ride. The Transit Police were absorbed into the NYPD anyway in 1995, but from 1993 – 1995 Long Island Railroad police recruits trained at the Transit Police Academy.

The Long Island Railroad Police Department was poised to enter the 21st century as a modern law enforcement agency with the goal of continuing its professional development. But it was not to be.

The Long Island Railroad was not the only commuter railroad operating in the New York Metropolitan Area. While the LIRR operated east from Manhattan out to the east end of Long Island, the Metro North Railroad operated north from Manhattan to New York's northern counties and parts of Connecticut. The Metro North Railroad also had their own police department.

It all began during the Fall of 1996. From October through December discussion were held between the unions representing the Long Island Railroad police officers and the Metro North police officers. Both agencies were part of the Metropolitan Transportation Authority, and the meetings with MTA Chairman E. Virgil Conway were to push for the twenty-year pension bill that was passed during the 1996 legislative session in Albany, but had been subsequently vetoed by Governor Pataki.

After numerous meetings, a topic other than pensions was brought to the table by the MTA Chairman. In 1995 The New York City Transit and Housing Police Departments had ceased to exist when they merged into the New York City Police Department. Over a year had passed and the merger of the three city police departments had been a success, so now Chairman Conway floated the idea of a merger between the LIRR Police and the Metro North Police.

Consequently, an agreement was reached on a merger of the two departments, which provided the membership of both departments with a twenty-year pension plan that would mirror the N.Y. State and Local Police and Fire Retirement System. The pension plan was administered by the MTA.

On January 1, 1998, the two departments officially became the Metropolitan Transportation Authority Police Department. On February 9, 1998, Thomas J. Savage of the New York City Transit was named Acting Chief of the MTA Police Department. Numerous promotions, assignments and consolidations shortly followed to better streamline the operations of the department. Chief Savage also budgeted for an additional twenty-five patrol cars for the department as well as upgrades to the communications system. Additionally, Chief Savage hired eleven new officers and they were assigned to the NYC Police Academy.

The MTA Police Benevolent Association opened its new office located at 134 Rockaway Avenue, Valley Stream, NY on September 10, 1998, closing the former PBA offices located in Hempstead and Yonkers. On September 14th, the first Executive Board meeting was held at the MTA PBA office.

Shortly thereafter the PBA and MTA tentatively agreed to a new collective bargaining agreement covering work rules, health care benefits, and equalization of pay for former Metro North officers with former LIRR officers. The agreement was overwhelmingly ratified by members of the PBA and also ratified by the MTA Board.

The Long Island Railroad Police Department was gone – or was it? I have learned from personal experience and through writing other books that the patch may change, but the mission goes on. I was a member of the Transit Police when the 1995 merger occurred. The day after the merger took place, nothing really changed. I was still working in the subway and people still referred to us as transit cops. In my first book in this series, when the members of the Brooklyn Bridge Police Department were absorbed into the City of Brooklyn Department, the cops still patrolled the bridge. Even though the patch is different the Long Island Railroad and its commuters is still protected by a dedicated department of skilled, professional police officers.

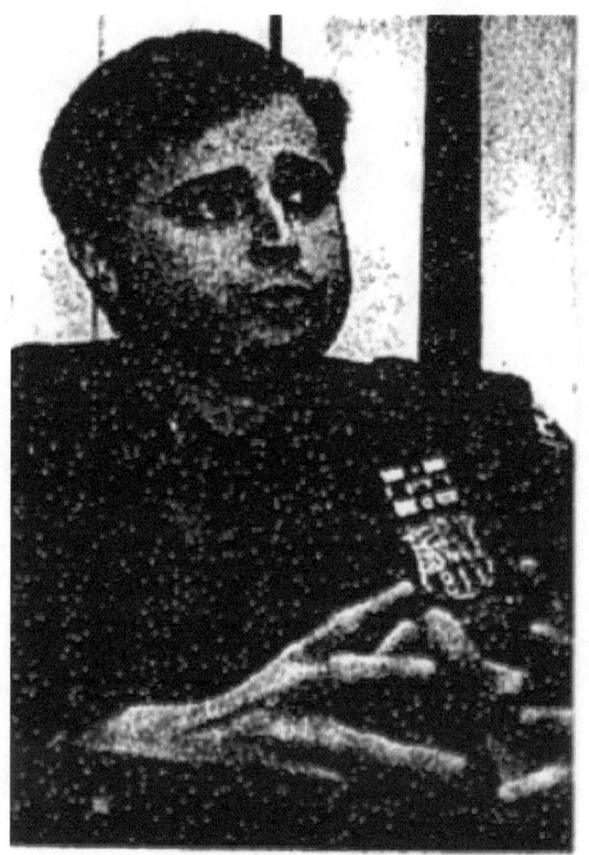

Eric Michelson for The New York Times

Andrew Roderick, the off-duty L.I.R.R. police officer who was at the Merillon Avenue station to pick up his wife Dawn, described his role yesterday in handcuffing and arresting the gunman.

Train Patrol

Watching for crossing violators

THE BEST: Honorees of the American Legion's Bellmore Post gathered at the recent Law and Order Awards ceremony.

Joseph B. Flynn
Chief of Police, Long Island Railroad

New York City
Transit Police Academy

GRADUATION CEREMONY
Recruit Class 93-1
York College, Jamaica, Queens

New York City Transit Police Department
Michael F. O'Connor, Chief of Police

July 8, 1993

Bibliography

1. Railroad Police.com - http://www.therailroadpolice.com/history

2. Berti, Adele, 185 Years of the Long Island railroad, Railway Technology, November 26, 2019

3. A DEMENTED SERVANT GIRL, The Brooklyn Daily Eagle, 9/3/1885, p4

4. CAPTAIN WOODS WANTED, The Brooklyn Daily Eagle, 9/2/1885, p4

5. THE ORIGINAL JACOBS, The Brooklyn Union, 9/2/1885, p2

6. CAPTAIN WOODS DISCHARGED, The Brooklyn Daily Eagle, 9/5/1885, p6

7. SIX CUTS ON HIS HEAD, The Brooklyn Daily Eagle, 6/7/1886, p6

8. TWO PLAIN DRUNKS, Brooklyn Times Union, 8/21/1888, p1

9. FIGHT ON A RAILROAD TRAIN, The Brooklyn Citizen, 7/29/1893, p1

10. MORE THEFTS, The Brooklyn Times Union, 12/9/1899, p15

11. UNTITLED, The Brooklyn Citizen, 4/14/1900, p9

12. UNTITLED, The Brooklyn Daily Eagle, 6/5/05, p8

13. OFFICER DE BOSCHE'S BRAVERY, Brooklyn Times Union, 5/2/03, p19

14. JAMES SARVIS, The Brooklyn Citizen, 6/5/05, p3

15. LIRR'S POLICE SYSTEM PROVES SIGNAL SUCCESS, The Brooklyn Citizen, 10/1/05, p18

16. UNTITLED, The Standard Union, 9/17/05, p24

17. LARRY SHOT HOLES IN DUMMY, The Brooklyn Daily eagle, 9/2/05, p2

18. LIRR ROBBED, The Brooklyn Citizen, 9/5/05, p5

19. SHOT IN LEG BY OFFICER, The Brooklyn Daily Eagle, 11/3/05, p24

20. L.I. RAILROAD SLEUTHS TRAINED TO THE MINUTE, The Brooklyn Daily Eagle, 1/23/09, p17

21. LIRR THIEVES CAUGHT WITH BLOODHOUNDS'AID, The Brooklyn Daily Eagle, 8/6/11, p15

22. THEY ARE SPECIAL PATROLMEN, The Brooklyn Daily eagle, 7/27/11, p14

23. GAYNOR MODIFIES SPECIAL POLICE RULE, The New York Times, 7/28/11, p7

24. RAILROAD SENDS A WARNING TO BOYS, Brooklyn Times Union, 10/30/12, p8

25. LONG ISLAND RR ASKS HELP OF SCOUTS, The Brooklyn Daily eagle, 6/25/14, p58

26. SAFETY FIRST CAMPAIGN, Brooklyn Times Union, 8/20/15, p2

27. OLD LI RAILROADER IS RETIRED AT 65, Brooklyn Times Union, 11/2/31, p88

28. LINDENHURST MAN DEFAMED PRESIDENT, the Brooklyn Daily Eagle, 9/26/18, p4

29. START FOR WORK LAND IN COURT, Brooklyn Times Union, 4/16/19, p9

30. MAN HELD AS PEEPER, Brooklyn TIMES Union, 11/1/19, p6

31. FATHER AND SON ARRESTED ON EACH OTHERS COMPLAINT, The Brooklyn Times Union, 9/29/19, p5

32. LIRR FREIGHT MEN ARE HELD, Brooklyn Times Union, 10/9/20, p6

33. LONG ISLAND RAILROAD INFORMATION BULLETIN, 9/30/24

34. LIRR OFFICIALS AWAIT WARRANTS AND INDICTMENTS. Brooklyn Times Union, 5/6/23, p2

35. BAKER-MAMMEN ARE EXONERATED IN CRASH, Brooklyn Times Union, 5/22/24, p11

36. RESERVES DECISION ON INDICTMENTS OF BAKER AND MANNEN, The Brooklyn Daily Eagle, 12/20/24, p3

37. LIRR INFORMATION BULLETIN 9/30/24
38. LIRR INFORMATION BULLETIN 2/20/24

39. HERO OF MONAHAN JUNCTION LIRR EMPLOYEE 25 YEARS, Brooklyn Times Union, 3/22/30, p12

40. LIRR INFORMATION BULLETIN 2/20/24

41. GATEMAN CRAVES MUSIC, TENANTS KICK TO POLICE, Nassau Daily review, 7/25/29, p4

42. Kathy Alexander, Legends of America, updated December 2021.

43. RAILWAY MAIL CLERK DESCRIBES HOW LONE BANDIT ROBBED HIS CAR OF SACK CONTAINING $10,000 CASH, The Brooklyn Times Union, 1/14/25, p1

44. LONG ISLAND RAILROAD REFUSES TO COMMENT ON MAIL CAR HOLD-UP, The Brooklyn Times Union, 1/14/25, p2

45. OFFICIALS SUSPECT GERALD CHAPMAN, Brooklyn Times Union, 1/14/25, p2

46. ARREST IS EXPECTED AT ONCE IN HOLDUP OF LONG ISLAND TRAIN, Brooklyn Times Union, 1/14/25, p1

47. HELD UP MAIL TRAIN FOR WIFESAYS CADOO, CAPTURED L.I. BANDIT, The Brooklyn Daily Eagle, 1/17/25, p1

48. TRACED BY AUTO CLUB, Brooklyn Times Union, 1/17/25, p35.

49. THRILLED BY THE ACT, UNAFRAID TRAIN ROBBER CADOO ASSERTS HE ENJOYED CHASE BY COPS, The Brooklyn Daily Eagle, 1/25/25, p19

50. SEEK TO RELEASE CADOO FROM JAIL, Brooklyn Times Union, 3/15/26, p3

51. ANNUAL REPORT OF THE ATTORNEY GENERAL OF THE UNITED STATES, 1928

52. PEOPLELEGACY
53. ENDS 50 YEARS WITH RAILROAD, The Standard Union, 11/2/31, p7

54. LONG ISLAND RAILROAD PRESENTS LOVING CUP TO SUPERINTENDENT OF POLIVR FOR SAFETY RECORD, The Brooklyn Citizen, 4/27/28, p3

55. CHIEF OF LONG ISLAND RAILROAD POLICE, The Brooklyn Citizen, 2/16/43, p3

56. COAL PILFERING YOUNGSTERS WORK IN SIGHT OF BOROUGH HALL WINDOWS, Brooklyn Times Union, 3/10/29, p47

57. LIRR COP HEADS POLICE EXAMS IN NASSAU SCHOOL, Brooklyn Times Union, 4/27/29, p28

58. 5 LIRR OFFICIALS UNDER $50,000 BAIL IN FATAL ACCIDENT, Brooklyn Daily Times, 2/29/24, p1

59. 5 BOYS HELD IN THEFT, The Brooklyn Daily Times, 10/23/26, p3

60. EX-COP ARRESTED AS RAIL BANDIT, Brooklyn Times Union, 11/20/30, p26

61. TOOT WHISTLE GANG REQUIEM, Brooklyn Times Union, 6/16/33, p3

62. AMITYVILLE COP ACCUSED BY GUARD, Brooklyn Times Union, 1/30/29, p49

63. GATETENDER HELD IN FATAL CRASH, Nassau Daily Review, 10/3/31, p1

64. SAY 6 WATCHMEN ABANDONED POSTS AT RAIL CROSSINGS, Brooklyn Times Union, 2/1/32, p66

65. RAIL HANDS SLEEP ON TRACKS NEAR THIRD RAIL WHILE DRUNK, Brooklyn Times Union, 7/18/29, p12

66. JUVENILE PRANKS KEPT LIRR POLICE BUSY, The Brooklyn Daily Eagle, 4/14/32, p28

67. CHIEF OF LONG ISLAND RAILROAD POLICE, The Brooklyn Citizen, 2/16/43, p3

68. Weddle, Bob, Long Island Railroad Posts Bond to free Motorman, Nassau Daily Review Star, 2/21/50, p

69. QUEENS GIRL ACCUSED OF DAMAGING SIGNAL EQUIPMENT OF LIRR, The Brooklyn Daily Eagle, 10/21/1950, p1

70. STATE OKS REMOVAL OF LIRR YARD GUARDS, the Brooklyn Daily Eagle, 11/21/52, p1

71. CRIPPLED LAD 13 TESTIFIES AT TRIAL OF $260,000 SUIT, The Brooklyn Daily Eagle, 5/10/51, p17

72. COPS HUNT BOY IN TWO ATTEMPTS TO DERAIL TRAIN, Brooklyn Daily Eagle, 2/24/53, p1

73. COMMUTER REVOLTS BALLING UP LIRR, The Brooklyn Daily Eagle, 8/7/53, p5

74. LIRR POLICE SHARPEN UNIFORMS AND TACTICS, The Patchogue Advance, 1/14/60, p1

75. Tallese, Gay, RAIL POLICE CHIEF USES A SPYGLASS, The New York Times, 6/9/62, p27

76. LAYOFFS PROTESTED BY LIRR POLICE, NY Times, 12/16/75, p42

77. LIRR POLICE PROTEST BAN ON GUNS, NY Times, 2/9/71, p24

78. HE TRACKS DOWN CRIME ON THE LIRR, NY Times, 1/14/1979, p2

79. THREE GO ON TRIAL ON LIRR ASSAULT, The New York Times, 9/22/70, p7

80. 3 L.I.R. POLICEMEN CLEARED OF ASSAULT, New York Times, 9/25/70, p6

81. $3.3 MILLION IS AWARDED WIDOW OF BEATING VICTIM, The New York Times, June 10, 1978

82. McQuiston, John T, LIRR ASSSIGNS ARMED POLICE TO COMMUTER CARS, The New York Times, 1/19/80, p25

83. LIRR TRAINS GET POLICE PATROLS, NY Times, 2/16/86, p11

84. Wilner, Frank, RAILWAY AGE May 23, 2014, Union boss may have LIRR in Checkmate

85. Levine, Richard, STRIKE ON L.I.R.R. STOPS ALL SERVICE; NEW TALKS TODAY, The New York Times, Jan. 19, 1987

86. Levine, Richard, JOINT PRESSURES BEHIND U.S. ACTION ON L.I.R.R, The New York Times, 1/29/78

87. OPERATION ZEBRA IS BAD NEWS FOR CAR THIEVES, The Suffolk County News, 10/12/89, p5

88. OFFICER WRITES THREE SUMMONES A DAY, The New York Times, 6/21/92, p191

89. Treaster, Joseph B, DEATH ON THE LIRR, NEW YORK TIMES, 12/9/93, p27

90. McQuiston, John T, WITNESSES RECALL TERROR OF LIRR SHOOTING, New York Times, 2/4/95, p11

91. Schemo, Diana, DEATH ON THE L.I.R.R, The New York Times, Dec. 9, 1993

92. Castillo, Alfonso, Experts: LIRR still vulnerable to mass shootings, but improvements made, alfonso.castillo@newsday.com, alfonso reports, December 6, 2018

93. McQuiston, John T, PATAKI SIGNS MEASURE GIVING POLICE A FREE RIDE ON LIRR, New York Times, 8/4/95, -p8

94. McQuiston, John T, PATAKI SIGNS MEASURE GIVING POLICE FREE RIDE ON LIRR, The New York Times, 8/4/95

95. Rabinowitz, Jonathan, LIRR AND CRITICS CLASH OVER EXTENT OF CRIME, New York Times, 4/30/94, p6

96. Barry, Dan, POLICE BREAK UP SUSPECTED BOMB PLOT IN BROOKLYN, New York Times, 8/1/97

97. BROOKLYN BOMBERS LINKED TO HAMAS, New York Herald, 8/1/97

98. William M. Moran and Daniel S. Weinberger, Authority of New York's Railroad Police Needs to Be Expanded, New York Law Journal, October 21, 2015

99. Guidelines for the Effective Use of Uniformed Transit Police and Security Personnel Final Report Prepared for: Transit Cooperative Research Program Transportation Research Board National Research Council Submitted by: Interactive Elements, Incorporated New York, New York May 1997